双语精华版

心灵鸡汤

[人生系列]

生命的彩虹

许俊农　主译

张文静　许蔚起　钱莉娜　余忠燕
李克议　黄跃勤　史晓薇　曹　青

Reaching for the Rainbow

Jack Canfield & Mark Victor Hansen 等 著

Chicken Soup for the Soul

安徽科学技术出版社

Health Communications, Inc.

国内独家　　　　亿册

图书在版编目(CIP)数据

心灵鸡汤：双语精华版. 生命的彩虹／（美）坎费尔德（Canfield, J.）等著；许俊农等译. -- 合肥：安徽科学技术出版社，2007.06
ISBN 978-7-5337-3781-8

Ⅰ. ①心… Ⅱ. ①坎… ②许… Ⅲ. ①英语－汉语－对照读物②故事－作品集－美国－现代 Ⅳ. ①H319.4：I

中国版本图书馆CIP数据核字(2007)第064520号

心灵鸡汤:双语精华版. 生命的彩虹
(美)坎费尔德(Canfield, J.)等著　许俊农译

出 版 人：朱智润
责任编辑：田　斌
封面设计：王国亮
出版发行：安徽科学技术出版社(合肥市政务文化新区圣泉路1118号
　　　　　出版传媒广场，邮编：230071)
网　　　址：www.ahstp.com.cn
E - mail：yougoubu@sina.com
经　　销：新华书店
排　　版：安徽事达科技贸易有限公司
印　　刷：合肥瑞丰印务有限公司
开　　本：889×1100　1/16
印　　张：14.25
字　　数：208千
版　　次：2007年9月第1版　2022年1月第2次印刷
定　　价：39.00元

作为美国大众心理自助与人生励志类的闪亮品牌，《心灵鸡汤》语言地道新颖，优美流畅，极富时代感。书中一个个扣人心弦的故事，深度挖掘平凡小事蕴藏的精神力量和人性之美，真率倾诉对生命的全新体验和深刻感悟，字里行间洋溢着爱心、感恩、信念、鼓励和希望。由于故事的蕴涵哲思深邃，豁朗释然，央视"百家讲坛"曾引用其作为解读援例。

文本的适读性与亲和力、故事的吸引力和感召力、内涵的人文性和震撼力，煲出了鲜香润泽的《心灵鸡汤》——发行40多个国家和地区，总销量上亿册的全球超级畅销书！

安徽科学技术出版社独家引进的该系列英文版，深得广大读者推崇与青睐，频登各大书店及"开卷市场零售监测系统"的畅销书排行榜，多次荣获全国出版发行业的各类大奖。

就学英语而言，本系列读物的功效已获莘莘学子乃至英语教学界的充分肯定。由于语篇的信度、效度符合标准化考试命题的质量要求，全国大学英语四级考试、全国成人本科学位考试的阅读理解真题曾采用其中的文章。

为了让更多读者受惠于这一品牌，我社又获国内独家授权，隆重推出双语精华版《心灵鸡汤》系列：英汉美文并蓄、双语同视面对照——广大读者既能在轻松阅读中提高英语水平，又能从中感悟人生的真谛，激发你搏击风雨、奋发向上的生命激情！

CONTENTS

目 录

目 录

目 录

Take That Chance!
抓住机遇!

If one advances confidently in the direction of his dreams and endeavors to live the life which he has imagined,he will meet with success unexpected in common hours.

Henry David Thoreau

如果一个人自信地向着他梦想的方向前进,努力去过他设想的生活, 他将会在平常的时刻获得意外的成功。

亨利·大卫·梭罗

They called it the "mud dive".You went down to fifty feet in the black,icy water in front of the Bayonne,New Jersey,U.S. Naval School and sank deep into the mud—and if you didn't panic,you could complete the rest of the rigorous course.

"You really don't have to make this dive,"said Dan Crawford,the Chief Petty Officer in charge,as I sat on the diving stool in my deepsea suit."You're just writing it up.We'll fill you in on how it is."

他们称这种运动为"潜泥"。在美国新泽西州的贝永海军学校的前面,你潜水下沉到50英尺深的黑暗而冰冷的水中, 深深地陷入淤泥里——假如你不恐慌的话,还可以完成这门严酷课程的其余部分。

"你真的不需要潜这次水," 当我穿着深海潜水服坐在潜水凳上时,负责接待的办公室主任丹·克劳福德说。"我们会告诉你那是怎么回事,而你只需把它详细写下来就行了。"

I already knew something about how it was by reading the diving manual."Bolt the helmet on,Chief,"I said,"before I change my mind."

In moments like that,one is inclined to wonder how he finds himself in such a situation.Six months before,I'd been sitting on a padded chair in an advertising agency with a steady salary and an expense account.Then the little painless lesion on my cheek was tested and turned out to be malignant.In the depths of my terror,I found resolve.

"Christine,"I said to my wife, "all my life I've wanted to try my hand at freelance writing.Now I'm going to give it a whirl—while I still have most of my face."

"I was wondering what it would take,"she said.

I quit my job,and we put $ 5,000—all our savings—down on a huge,decrepit old stone farmhouse in northern New Jersey. We bought a jeep for the family car and enrolled our three children in the local schools.We painted,caulked,roofed,glazed,dug and mowed our four acres of field.

Out back,attached to the barn,was an old chicken coop which,to my enchanted eye,had the makings of a writer's studio. With hammer and nails,I replaced the planks that had fallen askew.I cut back the blackberry bushes that were curling through the cracks and carted half a ton of well-seasoned chicken droppings off to the vegetable garden.I made my desk from a square of plywood which I set on saw horses,and we scrounged a rusty old coal stove from a neighbor's basement.I moved in an old captain's chair and my typewriter and was ready for business.This assignment—about the life of a Navy diving student—was one of my first stories.

I backed down into the water and,keeping a tight grip on the descending line,let myself sink into the gloomy depths.The ear pains began at once.In the dark I could feel the current washing my bulky diving suit against the pilings.The ear pains became excruciating—

双语精华版心灵鸡汤 ·

2

like two red-hot needles.I tried to clear my ears by swallowing.No luck.When my diving glove slipped on the slimy line,I began to sink fast,and one of my heavy diving boots jammed in a piling.Red wheels

通过阅读潜水手册，我已经了解到一些关于潜水是怎么回事的知识。"帮我扣上头盔吧，长官，"我说，"趁着我还没改变主意。"

在这种时刻，一个人往往对发现自己怎么会置身于这种处境感到惊奇。6个月前，我还坐在一家广告公司的软椅上，领着一份稳定的薪水，使用着报销账单。然而就在那时，我脸颊上那个微小的无痛的损伤经检查被确诊为恶性。我在深深的恐惧中作出了决定。

"克里斯汀，"我对妻子说，"我一辈子都想尝试自由写作。现在我要小试一下——在我的大部分脸还是完好的时候。"

"我想知道怎么干。"她说。

我辞去了工作。我们用全部的5 000美元积蓄买下了位于新泽西州北部的一栋巨大而古老的破旧农舍。我们购买了一辆吉普作家庭用车，并把我们的3个孩子送到当地的学校上学。我们粉刷墙壁，填补漏洞，修理屋顶，安装玻璃，我们给自己的四英亩地松土、割草。

屋后紧连着谷仓的是一个陈旧的鸡舍，这在我具有魔力的眼睛看来，有条件成为作家的工作室。我用锤子和钉子卸下已经歪斜的木板支架。我修剪了裂缝中弯曲生长的黑莓丛，用手推车装了半吨经过充分发酵的鸡粪，运到蔬菜园中。我在锯木架上锯好一块方形的厚木板，用它做了我的写字台。我们还从邻居的地下室里讨来一个生锈的煤球炉。我将一把旧船长椅和我的打字机搬进工作室，准备开始工作。这篇关于海军潜水生的生活作品就是我早先写的故事之一。

我背朝下沉入水中，紧紧握住缓缓下降的绳子，让自己沉入黑暗的深水中。我的耳朵开始感到疼痛。在黑暗中，我感到水流靠着拴绳子的桩冲刷我那宽大的潜水服。耳朵的疼痛开始变得难以忍受——仿佛有两根炽热的针在扎。我尝试通过做吞咽动作减轻耳朵的疼痛，但是没有效果。当潜水手套在泥泞的绳子上打滑时，我开始迅速下沉，这时，一只沉重的潜水靴卡在了一个桩上。红色的惊慌之轮在我脑中加快旋转。"拉我上去！"

of panic revved up in my head. "Bring me up! "I yelled into the helmet microphone.

Dan Crawford was chuckling when he lifted off the helmet. Something had been collecting in the back of my throat.I spat it out—bright red blood.

"You broke some blood vessels in your eustachian tubes,"Crawford said. "It happens all the time.But you did okay—you got to forty feet."

A national publication bought the story,and I was able to pay a lot of bills that had been backing up.But,most important,I had finally put into action the working philosophy that I had adopted for my new career:Pick the most demanding mission,go through it myself, then tell what happened.Henry David Thoreau wrote:

"The cost of a thing is the amount of what I will call life which is required to be exchanged for it,immediately or in the long run."

To me,this translated out:When a chance is offered,take it.

I've been doing this now for twenty-six years,and my chicken-coop studio is filled with mementos—trivial,even foolish,maybe,but all of them earned by Thoreau's kind of coin.There is the little blue-woolen diver's cap I wore for the mud dive.Those police handcuffs on the bookcase were used when I was writing a story about a boy who'd been kidnapped,tied up,and eventually driven and knocked out at high speed over back roads to a river.I wrote it nine times.Flat as stale beer.I asked Christine to tie me up,gag,handcuff and blindfold me and drive me over rough back roads on Schooleys Mountain and down to the Musconetcong River.She drove so fast that I was black and blue from bouncing around in the springless jeep.At one point,I thought I was going to swallow the gag.I was weak with relief when we stopped.But the exercise paid off.The kidnap sequence wrote itself;the story was published and,later,anthologized.

Then there is that lump of coal on the shelf I brought home as a souvenir of a mining story assignment in Hellier, Kentucky. Appalachian hospitality is as warm as a cherry-red stove, or it comes

我对着头盔中的麦克风大声呼叫。

丹·克莱福德吃吃地笑着帮我把头盔卸下来。我喉咙后部积聚了某种东西。我把它吐出来——鲜红的血。

"你的耳咽部的一些血管破裂了，"克莱福德说，"这是经常发生的。不过你做得不错——你潜到了40英尺深。"

一家全国性出版社买下了这个故事，于是我能够偿清逐渐累积的大堆债务。不过，最重要的是，我终于能把为我的新事业所采取的劳动哲学付诸行动:选择最苛刻的任务，亲自完成它，然后再叙述发生了什么。亨利·大卫·梭罗写道:

"一个东西的成本就是我称之为生活的量，它是你用当下或长久运行的生命的多少来交换的。"

我把这理解为:当机遇来临时，抓住它。

现在，我已经这样做了26年。我的鸡舍工作室里堆满了微不足道的甚至愚蠢的纪念品，它们都是由梭罗式的"钱币"挣来的。其中有我戴着它潜泥的小小蓝羊绒潜水帽。书柜上那副手铐是我在写一个关于被绑架小孩的故事时使用的。故事中，那个小孩被挟持之后，被捆了起来，最后被开车运走，他在车子以高速通过小路去河边的路上颠昏了过去。我把这篇故事写了九遍。平淡得就像变味的啤酒。于是，我让克里斯汀把我拴起来，嘴里塞上布条，把手铐起来，蒙上眼睛，让她开车带着我，从司古雷斯山上向山下的崎岖小路上直冲，一直冲到玛斯科奈特康河边。她把车开得那么快，以至我在毫无弹性的吉普车里颠簸的遍体鳞伤。有一刻，我都以为会把嘴里的布条吞下去。当车最终停下时，我觉得虚弱而轻松。不过我的演习得到了回报。这个绑架情节写得很逼真;这个故事出版了，不久又被收入了选集。

架子上还有一块煤，那是我在肯塔基的海里尔写一篇采矿的故事时，作为纪念品带回来的。阿帕拉契人的待客要不是像烧成樱桃红色的火炉

from the muzzle of a 32.20—depending on what you do. So when my truck was suddenly surrounded one night by a group of grim-faced men with rifles leveled,I didn't do anything but sit still and pray.My companion,a fellow I knew only as the Preacher,motioned me to keep quiet,climbed down,walked over to the moonshiners and talked with them.I don't know what he said,but I have a solid hunch he saved our lives.The men backed off and let us pass.

"Nightmare County,"my story about the Kentucky mining country,sold in the United States and Great Britain,and once again we caught up on our bills.

These were a few high points in our new life.But there is another side to Thoreau's coin.It involves not only the acceptance of risk but, very often,considerable belt-tightening.As author-critic Joseph Wood Krutch comments, "Security depends not so much upon how much you have as upon how much you can do without."One summer,for lack of funds,we did without a new pump and hauled our water by hand from the spring.We robbed the piggy bank when there was anything in it,and we froze so many string beans even the neighbors wouldn't have them.Twice I took pedestrian jobs to keep us going— once as a fund raiser,another time as a real estate salesman—but always,somehow,one more writing assignment came up,and I got back to the chicken coop.

And so my chicken coop is an incredible clutter of dis-reputable furniture,files full of research material and knickknacks from various corners of the earth.I write in my bare feet,wriggling my toes in a thick lambskin rug from Kenya.Scattered about the room in plain view are a jaguar skull from Ecuador,a bronze statue of Shiva from India and a chunk of lava I picked up one day when it was 115 degrees in the Rift Valley of East Africa.On bitter nights when the wind shrieks past the windows,I throw photographic slides on a screen that rolls down over the bookcase,and I am transported instantly to the Arctic,the Congo,the Pacific Islands.When I am beset by those ever-recurring moments of frustration and self-doubt,I lock the barn door,pick up my.22 caliber pistol and blast away at a target propped

那样温暖，就是像面对一把32.20毫米口径的枪口——这取决于你做什么。因此,当一天晚上我乘坐的拖拉机突然被一群面孔黝黑、举着步枪瞄准我们的人围住时,我只是静静地坐着祈祷。我的同伴示意我保持安静,我只知道这个同伴是个传教士。他爬下车,向这些做非法生意的人走去,和他们谈判。我不知道他说了些什么,但我有种坚定的预感——他会救我们的命。果然,那些人向后退开,放我们通过了。

我写的肯塔基矿区的故事《梦魇之郡》在美国和英国出版了,而我再一次清偿了债务。

以上这些是我们新生活中的少数高峰期,然而梭罗的硬币还有其另一面。这不仅涉及承受风险,还常常带来经济上的严重拮据。文学批评家约瑟夫·伍德·克鲁奇评论道:"安全在很大程度上既取决于你拥有多少资金,也取决于你在资金短缺时能做到什么。"有个夏天,由于缺少资金,我们没有购置新水泵,只能用手从泉中挑水。因为扑满里有一些钱,我们打碎了它,用了里面的钱。我们还冻了许多菜豆,而邻居却根本不吃这个。我两次干些跑腿的工作以维持生活——一次是当资金筹集者,一次是干真正的房地产销售商——可总是这样,不知何故,只要又想出一个新的写作计划,我就会回到鸡舍工作室去完成它。

我的鸡舍工作室是一个惊人混乱的地方,里面杂乱地堆着破旧的家具、写满调查数据资料的文件和从世界各地带来的小玩意儿。我赤足写作,把脚趾头蜷缩在一张从肯尼亚带来的羊皮毯里。向房间里随意四处一看,还可以发现一个美洲豹头骨,一尊来自印度的湿婆青铜神像和一大块熔岩。那熔岩是我有一天在华氏115度气温下于东非的大裂谷里拣到的。在严寒的夜晚,窗外寒风呼啸,我把摄像幻灯片投射在一个悬挂于书架的屏幕上,于是我的思绪立刻被带到北极、刚果和太平洋群岛。当我被那些总是反复发生的挫折和自我怀疑困扰的时候,我就锁上谷仓的门,拿起我22毫

in front of a huge heap of firewood forty feet away through the open office door.I use the two-handed police grip,lock my extended arms and squeeze down on the trigger as delicately as a safe cracker feeling for the combination.After all these years and nearly 12,000 rounds of ammunition,I can cluster six shots in a five-inch circle.Beats Valium!

Often at night,sitting in my office,I think of the greatest chance-taker I know.Christine deals in subtler areas of peril.For her it is not diving into chilly depths or facing gun-toting mountaineers.It is the much riskier business of bucking up the flagging spirit of another person—me.One morning after we moved to New Jersey,I looked at all the splendid homes along our road and an appalling thought hit me. "What,"I said, "will all these people think if I fail?"Christine laughed. "Well,they don't know our names,"she replied. "They'll proba-bly say, 'Hey,know what happened to that new family on the road? They starved to death.'"

Then there was the terrible moment when a publisher asked for changes in my first novel on which I'd been working for eight years—he wanted material taken out that was basic to what I was trying to say in the story.My first instinct was to protect the integrity of my work.On the other hand,I desperately wanted to see it in print.What to do?Christine told me.The next day I went back and,through gritted teeth,said to the publisher, "The book goes as is,or I'll try it else-where."It went,and *The Lion Pit* put our children through college.

Finally,there is one memento in my studio that has nothing to do with writing.It is a lucky nut,the fruit of a tree that grows along the Amazon.These nuts fall into the river,float out into the ocean and are eventually washed up in places like Daytona Beach,which is where I found mine.I value it because it reminds me of the retired philosophy professor who gave me the best tip on chance-taking of all.On a rough day when the surf was making the dunes shake,he would wade out into the fury,duck under a big roller and swim out to sea.

One morning I could stand it no longer.I asked him why.

米口径的手枪,通过开着的工作室门,向着架在40英尺外木柴堆前的靶子射击。我用需要双手操作的警用枪柄,把伸出的胳膊固定住,然后扣动扳机,敏感得像一个解密高手感觉锁的连接处。经过这些年的练习,耗费了12 000发子弹后,我能把6个弹孔聚集在一个5英寸的圆圈内。胜过安眠药!

晚上坐在办公室里,我常常想起我所知道的最伟大的冒险家。克里斯汀处在更微妙的险境中。对她来说,风险不在于潜进冰冷的深水中或面对持枪的山里人。更大的风险在于振作另一个人——我的委顿的情绪。我们搬到新泽西州后的一个早晨,我看着我们家所在的街道两旁那些都很华丽的房子,一种骇人的想法袭入心头。"人家会怎么看呢,"我说,"如果我失败了,所有这些人会怎么看我们?"克里斯汀大笑。"哦,他们不知道我们的名字,"她回答,"他们也许会说:'嘿,知道这条街上新来的那家发生了什么事吗? 他们饿死啦。'"

接着,可怕的时刻来临了。出版商要求我修改那本我整整写了8年的第一部小说——而他要删掉的材料对于我试图在故事中表达的内容是必不可少的。我的第一本能反应是保护我的作品的完整性,但另一方面,我又极其渴望看到它的出版。怎么办?克里斯汀告诉了我如此这般。第二天,我又回到了出版商那儿,我咬咬牙,对出版商说:"书就保持原样,否则我就到别处试试。"书保持原样出版了,这本《狮坑》的稿费供我们的3个孩子上完了大学。

最后,在我的纪念品中还有一件与写作无关的东西。那是一枚幸运果,一种生长在亚马逊河沿岸的树结的果实。这种坚果落入河中,随水流漂到海洋里,最后被冲上像戴托纳海滩这样的地方,我就在那儿找到了这枚坚果。我珍惜它,因为它使我想起那位退休的哲学教授,正是他在把握机遇方面给了我最好的建议。在暴风雨天气,当海浪让沙丘晃动时,他会涉水走进狂涛骇浪,突然潜入一个大浪,向海中游去。

一天早晨我再也忍不住了。我问他为什么这么做。

"大浪总让我恐惧,"他回答,"你看到我现在所做的正是我一辈子最

"Big waves have always terrified me,"he replied. "What you see me do now is something I've wanted to do all my life—but couldn't. Then I decided I would have to try it if it killed me.I waded out, watched one of those monsters gather itself until it towered up like a cliff and ducked under.When I surfaced behind it,I was king of the world! "

His eyes twinkled,"No man can hope to control his destiny. The best he can hope for is to control himself—one single act at a time. Those acts are like bricks in a wall.A wall made of such bricks is a man's character."

I believe this because,shortly afterward,I put it to the test. Driving up our road one winter night,I saw a tongue of fire billowing out of the back of the chicken coop.My first thought was for the one and only copy of a lengthy manuscript,which at that time,was nearly completed.I floored the accelerator,skidded into the driveway,left the car on the dead run,and a moment later was staring into a wall of flames floating between me and the desk where the manuscript lay in a plastic box.I realized in one of those rare flashes of insight,the chance we all must take once in our lives,I took a deep breath, squinted my eyes,lunged through the fire,grabbed the box and got out—all in one breath.Only then did I feel the pain in my hands from the nearly molten plastic.

The burn scars that I still carry probably make the best brick I'll ever put in my wall.

But I find I keep coming back to the words of Henry Thoreau concerning the true cost of a thing—anything.It is still basic to my writing career,and it is more;it has become the structure of my day-to-day existence.I have seen it work for others.When I see a person, young or old,rich or poor,who has a realizable dream for which he is willing to exchange a piece of his life,I know that person is building toward the highest goal he can attain.He is rising to a new level of being,using precious moments to mature and grow,to become stronger,braver,maybe even kinder and wiser.

I do not advocate rashness.Always look before you leap.But once

想做到——但是以前做不到的事。那时我决定试一下，哪怕这会让我死去。我走入水中，看着海浪如怪物般逐渐聚合变大,直到赫然耸立得像个悬崖时,我潜入其中。当我在它后面浮出水面,我似乎成了世界之王!"

他的眼睛闪着光:"没人能希望控制他的命运。他可以希望的最好东西是对自己的控制——每次控制一个单独的举动。这些举动就像墙上的砖。一座由这些砖组成的墙就构成了一个人的性格。"

我相信这点,因为在那之后不久,我就亲身试验了一回。一个冬天夜晚,当我开车沿街道回家时,我突然看到火舌舔舐着鸡舍工作室的背面。我的第一个念头就想到了那份唯一的已接近尾声的长剧的剧本。我把油门踩到底,在车道上猛地刹住车,离开车之后拼命地跑。刹那间,我瞪眼看着一堵火墙在我和书桌间晃动,书桌上摆着塑料盒,里面放着那个剧本。我在一闪念间意识到,人生必然要冒一次险的机会来了。我深吸一口气,眯上眼睛,猛冲进火中,抓住那个盒子冲了出来——这些都是一口气完成的。直到那时,我才感到抓着快要熔化的塑料盒子的手的痛。

我身上还存留着烧伤的痕迹,这也许是曾垒在我的性格之墙上最好的一块砖了。

但我发觉自己一直在回想亨利·梭罗所说的一个事物真正代价的话——任何事物都是这样。这依然是我写作事业的基础,但又不止这些;它已成为我日常生存的支柱。我曾看到它同样也对别人起作用。每当我看到一个人,年轻人或老年人,富有的或贫穷的,那些有一个可实现的梦想并为了这个梦想愿意用他们生命的一小部分来交换的人,我就知道他是在向着树立他所能达到的最高目标而努力。他正在向新的存在层次进展,他利用宝贵的时刻去成长、成熟,去变得更坚强、更勇敢,也许还更善良、更明智。

我并不提倡鲁莽。人总要三思而后行。可是一旦改变已经发生,就要

the move is made,be bold,take that chance! Never curse the dark. Light a candle,a match,anything,always remembering that the finest helping hand you are ever likely to find is the one attached to the end of your own arm.

Frank Harvey

大胆一些,抓住那个机遇!永远不要诅咒黑暗。点亮一支蜡烛吧,擦亮一根火柴或者任何东西,始终记住:最好的相助之手是长在你自己胳膊上的那只手。

Watching Me Go
看着我离开

What feeling is so nice as a child's hand in yours?
So small, so soft and warm, like a kitten huddling in the
shelter of your clasp.

Marjorie Holmes

握着孩子的手是一种多么好的感觉啊！那小小
的、柔软的、温暖的在你的拥握中就像一只小猫蜷缩
着、呵护着自己。

马乔里·福尔摩斯

The crayoned picture shows a first-grade boy with shoebox arms, stovepipe legs and tears squirting like melon seeds. The carefully printed caption reads, "I am so sad." It is my son Brendan's drawing-journal entry for September 19. Brendan cried his first day of school, dissolving at his classroom door like a human bouillon cube. The classroom jiggled with small faces, wet-combed hair, white Nikes and new backpacks. Something furry scuttled around in a big wire cage. Garden flowers rested on Mrs. Phillips's desk. Mrs. Phillips has halo

这幅蜡笔画的是一个一年级的小男孩，长着鞋盒似的胳膊，烟囱似的腿，眼泪像西瓜子一样四溅。精心书写的标题写道："我很伤心。"这是我儿子布郎杜9月19号记下的绘画日记。布郎杜在他上学第一天的日子里大哭不止，在教室门前几乎溶解成了肉汤方块。许多张小脸，蘸水梳过的头发，白色的耐克鞋和崭新的背包在教室里摇晃。有毛茸茸的东西从大的电线笼子里逃出来。盆栽花放在菲力普太太的书桌上。菲力普太太在学校声誉

status at our school.She is a kind,soft-spoken master of the six-year-old mind.But even she could not coax Brendan to a seat.Most kids sat eagerly awaiting Dick and Jane and two plus two.Not my Brendan.His eyes streamed,his nose ran and he clung to me like a snail on a strawberry.I plucked him off and escaped.

It wasn't that Brendan didn't like school.He was the kid at the preschool Christmas concert who knew everyone's part and who performed "Jingle Bells"with operatic passion.Brendan just didn't like being apart from me.We'd had some good times,he and I,in those preschool years.We played at the pool.We skated on quiet morning ice.We sampled half the treat tray at weekly neighborhood coffee parties.Our time together wasn't exactly material for a picture book, but it was time together.And time moves differently for a child.

Now in first grade,Brendan was faced with five hours of wondering what I was doing with my day.Brendan always came home for lunch,the only one of his class not to eat at his desk.But once home, fed and hugged,a faraway look of longing would crease his gentle brow—he wanted to go back to school to play! So I walked him back, waited with him until he spotted someone he knew,then left.He told me once that he watched me until he couldn't see me anymore,so I always walked fast and never looked back.One day when I took Brendan back after lunch,he spied a friend,kissed me good-bye and scampered right off.I went,feeling pleased for him,celebrating his new independence,his entry into the first-grade social loop.And I felt pleased for myself,a sense of well-being and accomplishment that I, too,had entered the mystic circle of parents whose children separated easily.

Then—I don't know why—I glanced back.And there he was.The playground buzzed all around him,kids everywhere,and he stood,his chin tucked close,his body held small,his face intent but not sad, blowing me kisses.So brave,so unashamed,so completely loving, Brendan was watching me go.

No book on mothering could have prepared me for that quick,

很好。对于一个6岁的孩子来说,她是一个和蔼、说话温柔的人。但就是她,也不能说服布郎杜坐下来。大多数孩子坐在那急切的等着说故事和做数学题。但我的布郎杜没有。他泪眼朦胧,涕泗滂沱,紧紧地贴着我就像一只蜗牛扒在草莓上。我挣脱他逃走了。

其实布郎杜并不是不喜欢学校,他在学前班的时候参加过圣诞音乐会,知道每一个人的表演部分,而且用一种歌剧的热情演唱着"铃儿响叮当"。布郎杜仅仅是不想离开我。我们,我和他,在学前班的时候曾经有过许多美好的时光。我们在河边玩耍。我们在宁静的清晨溜冰。我们在每周的邻里咖啡宴会上选取一半的招待盘子。我们在一起的日子并不完全是像图画书画的那样,但我们切切实实在一起。对于孩子来说,时间总是过得很快。

现在在一年级的教室里,布郎杜每天都要面对着5个小时想象着我在这一天里做些什么。布郎杜总是回家吃午饭,他是他们班唯一的一个不在教室课桌上用餐的。但是一旦回家,吃饱了,与我拥抱后,一种强烈的渴望就会封锁他的眉头——他想回学校玩!于是我就送他回去,和他一起等着,直到他看到了他熟悉的人,然后离开。有一次他告诉我他会目送我直到看不见我为止,所以我总是走得很快而且从不回头。然而有一天我午饭后送布郎杜回去,他很快看到了一个朋友,他匆匆和我说再见,立刻跑开了。我为他感到高兴,为他取得的新的独立,进入了一年级的社交圈中感到庆贺。我同时也为自己感到高兴,一种满足感和成就感涌上心头,我自己也踏入了一个神秘的圈子,在那儿,家长会适应和孩子的轻易别离。

然后我不知道为什么——我回头看了一下。他正在那里。孩子们在他的周围,整个操场喧闹着,他站在那儿,下巴向里收着,身体缩得很小,表情很专注但没有伤心,他向我抛来飞吻。那么勇敢,毫不羞涩,那么充满爱意,布郎杜看着我离开。

没有任何教如何做母亲的书能让我通过那迅速粗糙的一瞥进入孩子

raw glimpse into my child's soul.My mind leaped fifteen years ahead to him packing boxes and his dog grown old and him saying,"Dry up, Mom.It's not like I'm leaving the country."In my mind,I tore up the card every mother signs saying she'll let her child go when he's ready.I looked at my Brendan,his shirt tucked in,every button done up,his toes just turned in a bit,and I thought,*Okay,you're six for me forever.Just try to grow up,I dare you.*With a smile I had to really dig for,I blew him a kiss,turned and walked away.

Diane Tullson

的灵魂。我的思绪跳跃到15年以后,他正在打包行李,他的狗也长大了,他对我说:"擦干眼泪,妈妈。我并不是要离开这个国家呀。"在我的脑海中,我撕毁了那个每个妈妈都签名说她会在她的小孩准备好后,让他离开的卡片。我看着我的布郎杜,他的衬衫塞的很整齐,每一个纽扣都系的很好,他的脚趾有一点向里弯,我想:"好吧,你对我来说永远都是6岁,你敢长大。"我的脸上浮现出一丝值得我去回味的微笑,我给了他一个飞吻,然后转过身,走开了。

Daddy's Little Girl
爸爸的女儿

"Will you tell Daddy for me?"

That was the worst part.At seventeen,telling my mom I was pregnant was hard enough,but telling my dad was impossible.Daddy had always been a constant source of courage in my life.He had always looked at me with pride,and I had always tried to live my life in a way that would make him proud.Until this.Now it would all be shattered.I would no longer be Daddy's little girl.He would never look at me the same again.I heaved a defeated sigh and leaned against my mom for comfort.

"I'll have to take you somewhere while I tell your father.Do you understand why?"

"Yes,Mama."Because he wouldn't be able to look at me,that's why.

"你会帮我告诉爸爸吗？"

那是件难以启齿的事。17岁，我告诉妈妈自己怀孕的事情已经够难的了，可是还要再告诉我爸爸，这简直是不可能的事情。爸爸一直是我生命中勇气的源泉，他很骄傲有我这样一个女儿，而且我也一直努力让他以我为荣。直到发生了这件事情。现在，一切都被我毁了。我已不再是爸爸的乖女儿，他再也不会像以前那样看我了。我悲伤地叹了口气，靠在妈妈的身上寻求安慰。

"我告诉你爸爸这件事的时候，你得去别的地方待着。你知道我为什么要你这么做吗？"

"我知道，妈妈。"因为他没法在听这件事情时面对我，这就是原因。

那天晚上我去了我们的教堂，和鲁牧师一起待着，那时候只有和他待

I went to spend the evening with the minister of our church, Brother Lu,who was the only person I felt comfortable with at that time.He counseled and consoled me,while Mom went home and called my dad at work to break the news.

It was all so unreal.At that time,being with someone who didn't judge me was a good thing.We prayed and talked,and I began to accept and understand the road that lay ahead for me.Then I saw the headlights in the window.

Mom had come back to take me home,and I knew Dad would be with her.I was so afraid.I ran out of the living room and into the small bathroom,closing and locking the door.Brother Lu followed and gently reprimanded me.

"Missy,you can't do this.You have to face him sooner or later.He isn't going home without you.C'mon."

"Okay,but will you stay with me?I'm scared."

"Of course,Missy.Of course."I opened the door and slowly followed Brother Lu back to the living room.Mom and Dad still hadn't come in yet.I figured they were sitting in the car,preparing Dad for what to do or say when he saw me.Mom knew how afraid I was.But it wasn't fear that my father would yell at me or be angry with me.I wasn't afraid of him.It was the sadness in his eyes that frightened me.The knowledge that I had been in trouble and pain,and had not come to him for help and support.The realization that I was no longer his little girl.

I heard the footsteps on the sidewalk and the light tap on the wooden door.My lip began to quiver,opening a new floodgate of tears, and I hid behind Brother Lu.Mom walked in first and hugged him, then looked at me with a weak smile.Her eyes were swollen from her own tears,and I was thankful she had not wept in front of me.And then he was there.He didn't even shake Luther's hand, just nodded as he swept by,coming to me and gathering me up into his strong arms, holding me close as he whispered to me,"I love you.I love you,and I will love your baby,too."

He didn't cry.Not my dad.But I felt him quiver against me.I knew

在一起我才觉得安心。他给我忠告,也安慰我,同时妈妈回家给正在上班的爸爸打电话,告诉他这个消息。

这一切像是有点不真实。不过当时,和一个不会评论我是非对错的人在一起,感觉很好。我们祈祷着交谈着,我渐渐开始接受并了解铺在我前方的是一条什么样的路。接着,我透过窗户玻璃看到了汽车的前车灯。

妈妈已经回来了,接我回家,我还知道爸爸会和她一起来。我害怕极了,我跑出客厅,躲进狭小的浴室,把门关上,锁了起来。鲁牧师一路跟随我来到浴室,小声地谴责我。

"小丫头,别这样。你迟早都要面对你爸爸的。你不回家他也不会回去的。来,别这样。"

"好吧,可是你会陪我一起吗？我好害怕。"

"当然了,小丫头。我当然会陪你一起。"我打开门,跟在鲁牧师身后,慢慢地回到了客厅。妈妈和爸爸还没有进门。我琢磨着他们一定坐在车里,爸爸正在想见到我以后该做些什么或是说些什么吧。妈妈知道我有多么害怕,我不是害怕爸爸见到我会冲我大呼小叫或是生我的气。我不害怕爸爸,我害怕的是他眼神里流露出的悲伤失望,害怕的是我深陷烦恼和痛苦而没有向他寻求帮助和支持这样一个悲哀的事实, 害怕的是我意识到我不再是他的宝贝女儿。

我听见过道上的脚步声,看到了木头门上的灯光。我躲在鲁牧师的身后,嘴唇开始颤抖,泪如雨下。妈妈先走了进来,和鲁牧师拥抱了一下,然后看着我,脸上带着一丝微笑。她的眼睛都哭肿了,我很感激她没有当着我的面掉眼泪。接着是爸爸,他甚至没有和鲁牧师握手,只是对他点了点头,便直接朝我走来,用他强有力的臂膀把我紧紧拥住,小声地对我说:"我爱你,宝贝。我爱你,我也会爱你的孩子。"

爸爸没有哭,我爸爸是不哭的。但是我感觉到他在发抖。我知道他强

it took all of his control not to cry,and I was proud of him for that. And thankful.When he pulled back and looked at me,there was love and pride in his eyes.Even at that difficult moment.

"I'm sorry,Daddy.I love you so much."

"I know.Let's go home."And home we went.All of my fear was gone.There would still be pain and trials that I could not even imagine.But I had a strong,loving family that I knew would always be there for me.Most of all,I was still Daddy's little girl,and armed with that knowledge,there wasn't a mountain I couldn't climb or a storm I couldn't weather.

Thank you,Daddy.

Michele Campbell

忍着没有哭出来,我为爸爸感到无比自豪并且感激万分。当他松手注视着我的时候,尽管在这样艰难的时刻,他的眼里仍然充满了爱和骄傲。

"对不起,爸爸。我真的好爱你。"

"我知道。我们回家吧。"我们回到了家。我没有了担心害怕,尽管我知道一定还会有我想象不到的痛苦和磨炼在等着我。但是我知道我有一个坚强的、充满爱心的家庭在永远支持着我。最重要的是,我仍然是爸爸的宝贝女儿,认清了这样的事实,没有任何一座山我不能跨越的,没有任何风雨是我不能度过的了。

谢谢你,爸爸。

Accused of Plagiarism— My Highest Compliment
剽窃——对我的最高赞誉

It seems to me that all writers,including those who deserve to be classified as geniuses,need encouragement,particularly in their early years.I always knew I could write,but that just meant I wrote a little better than the other kids in my classes.That I might one day write well enough to derive income from my efforts,oddly enough,never occurred to me during my grade school and high school years.

There was a particular teacher at Hyde Park High School in Chicago,Illinois,who,simply by concentrating her attention on me, made me believe that I might be able to master the knack of writing well enough to consider the craft as a profession.Her name was Marguerite Byrne,and she taught English,which,of course,involved writing skills.Whatever instruction she shared with me was exactly the same as all her other students enjoyed,but the difference was she encouraged me to begin the process of submitting things I was writing,in

在我看来,似乎所有的作家都需要鼓励,包括那些应当被划为天才的作家在内,尤其在他们写作的初期。我一直知道自己能写,但那只意味着我可以比班上的其他孩子写得稍好一点而已。也许,有一天我能写得好到可以通过自己的努力取得收入,这个想法说来也怪,在我小学和中学时期却从未在脑海中浮现过。

在伊利诺伊斯州芝加哥市的海德公园高级中学,有这样一位特别的老师,她仅仅通过把她的注意力放在我身上,让我相信自己能够掌握写作诀窍,足以把写作作为职业来考虑。她叫玛格丽特·伯恩,教英语,当然也包括写作技巧。她教授给我的知识完全和其他同学一样,不同的只是她鼓

生命的彩虹

21

that day,chiefly poems.

To my surprise the *Chicago Tribune* not only thought enough of several of my verses to publish them,but also paid me—inadvertently—the highest compliment a fledgling author can receive.The editor wrote a confidential letter to Miss Byrne,asking her to see,if by chance,one of her students—a certain Stephen Allen—might be guilty of plagiarism.The editor's suspicions had been aroused because,he was kind enough to say,he found it hard to believe that a seventeen-year-old could create material on such a professional level.

When Miss Byrne shared the letter with me,I was ecstatic! It was wonderfully encouraging.Maybe I really was a writer,I thought.

Miss Byrne also encouraged me to enter a contest sponsored by the CIVITAN organization.The assignment was to write an essay titled "Rediscovering America".I was literally astonished when I received a letter saying that I was the winner of the contest.The prize was a check for one-hundred dollars and an invitation to an all-the-trimmings banquet at a hotel in downtown Chicago.

My mother,at the time,was not even aware that I was interested in writing,or if she had somehow found out about it,she took little notice.When I arrived back home that evening,she didn't ask how the evening had gone.I placed the one-hundred-dollar check on the breakfast table where she would see it when she awoke in the morning—and went immediately to bed.

This scenario demonstrates the tremendous importance of giving young people caring attention and encouraging them to develop and practice such gifts as they might have.Years later,I was able to repay my debt to Marguerite Byrne by dedicating one of my books,Wry on the Rocks—*A Collection of Poems*, to her.

On the other hand,without encouragement talented students may never be motivated to learn,develop skills,or reach their full potential.

For example,at the same high school,there was a teacher whose Spanish language classes I attended but from whom I,unfortunately, learned very little simply because of the woman's cold,sarcastically critical attitude.She seemed to know nothing about encouraging students,and she was gifted at speaking contemptuously of those of us

励我开始把写的作品投稿,那时主要是诗歌。

让我惊喜的是,《芝加哥论坛报》不仅充分考虑发表我的一些诗行,还不经意地给予我——一个初出茅庐的作家能够得到的最高赞誉。该报编辑给伯恩小姐写了一封绝密信,让她看看她的一个名叫斯蒂芬·艾伦的学生是否偶然地涉嫌剽窃。那位编辑十分友善地说,他很难相信一个17岁的少年能写出这样有专业水准的作品。

当伯恩小姐把这封信拿给我看时,我欣喜若狂! 这真是很棒的鼓励。我想,也许我真的可以成为作家。

伯恩小姐还鼓励我参加一个由西维坦俱乐部发起的竞赛。任务是写一篇题为"重新发现美国"的文章。当我收到一封告知我是这次竞赛的获胜者的函件时,我着实吃了一惊。奖品是一张100美元的支票和一封出席位于芝加哥市中心的一家旅馆里的盛宴的邀请函。

我母亲那时根本没有意识到我对写作感兴趣, 即使她隐隐约约发现了这点,也没在意。那天晚上我回到家时,她没问我这个晚上是怎么过的。我把100美元的支票放在早餐桌上——这样她早上一醒来就能看见了——然后立即去睡觉了。

我的经历证明了给予年轻人关注, 鼓励他们发展和实现自己天分的重大意义。几年以后,我终于能够通过题献我的一本书给伯恩小姐的方式来偿还欠她的债务,题献的书是《诗集:歪斜的岩石》。

反之,若没有鼓励,有天分的孩子也许永远都没有动力去学习,去发展技能,去发挥自己的最大潜能。例如,在同一所高中,还是在那所高中,有一位教西班牙语的老师。我上她的课,可惜却没学到多少东西,仅仅因为这位女士冷嘲热讽的讥刺的批评态度。她似乎从不知道鼓励学生,而她在轻蔑地数落那些学得不够快的学生方面又似乎特别有天分。她的消极

who were not learning fast enough.Her negativism drove me away. Partly because of this teacher's negative influence,I am not fluent in Spanish today.

You see,I had already learned that one can derive instructive benefit from bad examples—by avoiding that behavior.   Alcoholism was a serious problem in my mother's family.As a result of having seen enough examples of alcoholic excess in my childhood,I have never had any interest in drinking.The same applies to smoking.My poor mother was a two-pack-a-day victim of nicotine addiction,and because of the endless clouds of smoke,the coughing,the overfilled ashtrays,and the ugly smell of cigarette smoke in the house and in my clothing,I have never smoked a cigarette in my life.

Again,young writers need to be encouraged.Because of Miss Byrne's influence,I have enjoyed a lifetime of writing books,songs,and TV scripts.And guess what?I haven't plagiarized a single word of any of it.

Steve Allen

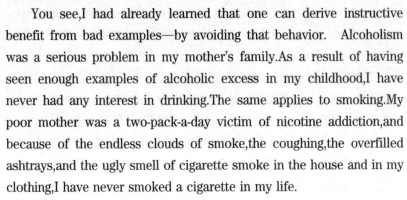

态度让我畏而远之。部分由于这位老师的消极影响,直到今天我讲西班牙语还不很流利。

你们知道,我已经懂得通过避免某种行为而从其反面事例中汲取教训。酗酒在我母亲家族里是一个严重问题。正由于我童年时看过太多饮酒过量的例子,以致我从来对饮酒毫无兴趣。这也同样适用于吸烟。我可怜的妈妈是个一天抽两包烟的染上烟瘾的受害者,无休止的烟雾缭绕,不间断的咳嗽,堆满烟头的烟灰缸,飘荡在房间里和沾染在我衣服上难闻的香烟味,这一切令我一生从未吸过一支烟。

再强调一下,年轻的作者需要鼓励。由于伯恩小姐的影响,我一生快乐地写书,填歌词,创作电视剧本。猜猜看是什么激励着我?我从未抄袭过哪怕一个字。

More Than a Friend
岂止是朋友

We may find some of our best friends in our own blood.

Theodore Roosevelt

我们也许能在自己的家族中找到最好的朋友。

西奥多·罗斯福

Louisville,Kentucky,is a place where basketball is an important part of life,and taking my son to an NBA exhibition game is very special.Little did I realize how special the evening was going to be! It was a biting winter cold that was blowing some mean wind,as Josh held my hand as we crossed the Kentucky Fairgrounds parking lot headed for famous Freedom Hall.Being eight years old,he still felt it was okay to hold his father's hand,and I felt grateful,knowing that these kind of moments would pass all too soon.

The arena holds nineteen-thousand-plus fans,and it definitely looked like a sellout as the masses gathered.We had been to many a University of Louisville basketball game and even a few University of

肯塔基的路易斯维尔是这样一个地方，在那里篮球是生活的重要组成部分，带着儿子去看一场NBA的表演赛无疑是非常别致的事。然而我并没有意识到那个晚上将会如此特殊！那天寒风刺骨。乔希拉着我的手，我们穿过肯塔基赛场的停车场，前往著名的自由大厅。我感到欣慰的是,8岁的乔希依然不在意握着爸爸的手,我知道,这种时光将很快会消逝。

这个赛场可以容纳一万七千多球迷,观众到齐后,一眼望去绝对是满座。我们曾在这个神圣的大厅里观看过许多路易斯维尔大学队的篮球比

生命的彩虹

Kentucky games in this hallowed hall, but the anticipation of seeing Michael Jordan and the Chicago Bulls against the Washington Bullets (with ex-University of Louisville star Felton Spencer) made our pace across the massive parking lot seem like a quick one, with lots of speculation about how the game was going to go.

The turnstile clicked and Josh hung on to his souvenir ticket stub like he had just won the lottery! Climbing the ramps to the upper elevation seemed more an adventure than a chore, as we got to the upper-level seats of the "true"fans. Before we knew it, the game was underway and the battle had begun. During a time out, we dashed for the mandatory hot dog and Coke and trotted back so that we wouldn't miss a single layup or jump shot. Things were going as expected until halftime. I started to talk to some friends nearby when there was a tug on my sleeve, my arm was pulled over by a determined young Josh Frager, and he began putting a multicolored, woven yarn bracelet around my wrist. It fit really well, and he was really focused intently as he carefully made a double square knot to keep it secure (those Scouting skills really are handy). Being a Scoutmaster with a lot of teenage Scouts, I recognized the significance of the moment, and wanting him to be impressed with my insightful skills, I looked him squarely in the eyes, smiled the good smile, and told him proudly how I knew this was a "friendship bracelet"and said, "I guess this means we are friends."

Without missing a beat, his big brown eyes looked me straight in the face, and he exclaimed, "We're more than friends... You're my dad!"

I don't even remember the rest of the game.

Stanley R. Frager

赛,甚至还看过一些肯塔基大学队的篮球赛。不过,亲眼见到迈克尔·乔丹和芝加哥公牛队对抗有非路易斯维尔大学队的明星费尔顿·斯宾赛在内的华盛顿子弹队的期望还是让我们加快了脚步,我们匆匆穿过巨大的停车场,边走边推测着这场比赛将会怎样进行。

咔嗒一声,乔希紧握纪念票根通过检票机的十字转门,那高兴劲儿仿佛中了头彩!我们爬上斜坡到达高处那"真正的"球迷座位的历程绝非易事,倒更像是一场冒险。比赛在不经意间就进行了。战斗打响了!在一次叫停时,我们冲出去取配给的热狗和可乐,又小跑回来,以免错过哪怕一个简单的上篮动作或跳投。

上半场一切都如预期的那样进行着。我开始和邻近的几个朋友谈话。忽然,我的袖子被拉了一下,接着胳膊被执著的小乔希·弗兰戈拽过去,他开始把一个彩色纱线编织的手链绕到我手腕上。这手链的确很合适,乔希专心致志,他细心地打了个双层平结使它更加牢固(那些童子军的手艺唾手可得)。然而,作为一个带领许多少年童子军队员的童子军团长,我认识到这一特定时刻的意义。我希望自己富于洞察力的见解能给他留下深刻印象,于是坦诚地望着他的眼睛,带着善意的微笑自豪地告诉他,我怎么知道这是个"友谊手链",还说道:"我猜想这手链意味着我们是朋友了。"乔希那大大的棕色眼睛直视着我的脸,他拍了我一下,大声说:"我们岂止是朋友,你是我爸爸呀!"

我连那场比赛后来是怎样进行的都记不得了。

Ronny's Book
罗尼的书

At first glance,Ronny looked like every other kid in the first-grade classroom where I volunteered as the Reading Mom.Wind-blown hair,scuffed shoes,a little bit of dirt behind his ears,some kind of sandwich smear around his mouth.

On closer inspection,though,the layer of dirt on Ronny's face,the crusty nose,and the packed grime under his fingernails told me he didn't get dirty at school.He arrived that way.

His clothes were ragged and mismatched,his sneakers had string for laces,and his backpack was no more than a plastic shopping bag.

Along with his outward appearance,Ronny stood apart from his classmates in other ways,too.He had a speech impediment,wasn't reading or writing at grade-level and had already been held back a year,making him eight years old in the first grade.His home life was a shambles with transient parents who uprooted him at their whim.He had yet to live a full year in any one place.

I quickly learned that beneath his grungy exterior,Ronny possessed a spark,a resilience that I'd never seen in a child who faced such tremendous odds.

I worked with all the students in Ronny's class on a one-on- one basis to improve their reading skills.Each day,Ronny's head twisted around as I came into the classroom,and his eyes followed me as I set up in a corner,imploring,"Pick me! Pick me! "Of course I couldn't pick him every day.Other kids needed my help,too.

On the days when it was Ronny's turn,I'd give him a silent nod, and he'd fly out of his chair and bound across the room in a blink.He

sat awfully close—too close for me in the beginning,I must admit—
and opened the book we were tackling as if he were unearthing a
treasure the world had never seen.

I watched his dirt-caked fingers move slowly under each letter as
he struggled to sound out "Bud the Sub".It sounded more like "Baw
Daw Saw"when he said it because of his speech impediment and his

在我作为志愿者当阅读妈妈的那个班里，罗尼乍看之下与任何其他
一年级学生差不多。他头发乱蓬蓬的，穿着鞋底磨损的鞋子，耳朵根后面
有一点污迹，嘴巴周围沾着三明治的碎屑。

但靠近观察，罗尼脸上的脏已经积成了层，鼻子上的尘埃、塞满污垢
的指甲却说明他不是在学校里弄脏的。他是生性如此。

他衣衫褴褛，搭配失谐，运动鞋的鞋带用绳子代替，书包只是一个塑
料购物袋。

除了外表不同，罗尼还在其他方面和班上同学不一样。他有语言障
碍，没有达到小学的读写水平，他已经留了一级，到8岁还在上一年级。他
的家庭生活一团糟，代理家长一心血来潮就把他赶出家门。直到现在，他
还不曾在谁家住满一年。

我很快发现，在罗尼邋遢的外表下有一股活力，一种适应力，这种适
应力我从未在一个承受如此巨大差异的孩子身上看到。

我以一对一的形式帮助罗尼班里所有同学提高阅读能力。每当我一
踏进教室，罗尼的脑袋就扭过来，眼睛随着我转，看着我在角落里坐下，那
眼神仿佛在恳求："叫我！叫我呀！"当然，我不可能天天叫他，因为其他孩
子也需要我的帮助。

轮到一对一帮助罗尼的日子，我会无声地对他点点头，他便飞快地离
开座椅，一眨眼工夫就连蹦带跳地穿过整个教室，来到我身边。他坐得离
我相当近——我得承认，开头我觉得过于近了——小心翼翼地打开我们
要阅读的书，那神情仿佛在发掘稀世之宝。

我看着他用满是污垢的手指在每个字母下慢慢移动，一边努力发出
"拨德萨"，当他念的时候，由于发音障碍和认识字母表的困难，听上去却

difficulty with the alphabet.

Each word offered a challenge and a triumph wrapped as one; Ronny painstakingly sounded out each letter,then tried to put them together to form a word.Regardless if "ball"ended up as"Bah-lah"or "bow", the biggest grin would spread across his face,and his eyes would twinkle and overflow with pride.It broke my heart each and every time.I just wanted to whisk him out of his life,take him home, clean him up and love him.

Many nights,after I'd tucked my own children into bed,I'd sit and think about Ronny.Where was he?Was he safe?Was he reading a book by flashlight under the blankets?Did he even have blankets?

The year passed quickly and Ronny had made some progress but hardly enough to bring him up to grade level.He was the only one who didn't know that,though.As far as he knew,he read just fine.

A few weeks before the school year ended,I held an awards cere-mony.I had treats,gifts and certificates of achievement for everyone: Best Sounder-Outer,Most Expressive,Loudest Reader,Fastest Page-Turner.

It took me awhile to figure out where Ronny fit;I needed some-thing positive,but there wasn't really much.I finally decided on"Most Improved Reader"—quite a stretch,but I thought it would do him a world of good to hear.

I presented Ronny with his certificate and a book—one of those Little Golden Books that cost forty-nine cents at the grocery store checkout.Tears rolled down his cheeks,streaking the ever-permanent layer of dirt as he clutched the book to his chest and floated back to his seat.I choked back the lump that rose in my throat.

I stayed with the class for most of the day;Ronny never let go of the book,not once.It never left his hands.

A few days later,I returned to the school to visit.I noticed Ronny on a bench near the playground,the book open in his lap.I could see his lips move as he read to himself.

His teacher appeared beside me."He hasn't put that book down

更像"博道骚"。

每个单词对他都是挑战,也是胜利;罗尼努力地发出每个字母的音,然后试着把它们组合构成一个单词。尽管他把"球"念成了"汽—油"或"桥",但每读一次都会在脸上绽放出一朵最大的笑容,他的眼睛闪着光,充满了自豪之情。这种情景每一次都让我心碎。我只想赶快让他远离他的生活,带他回家,把他洗干净,好好地爱他。

有许多夜晚,当我把自己孩子安顿入睡后,我会坐下来想到罗尼。他在哪儿?他安全吗?他是否借着手电光在毛毯里看书呢?然而他是否有毛毯呢?

那年过得很快,罗尼取得了一些进步,但仍未达到小学水平。只不过他自己是唯一一个不知道这种情况的人。就他而言,他知道的只是自己读得很好。

几周后,我在学年结束前举行了一次颁奖典礼。我为每个人都准备了赠品、礼物和学习成就证书:发音最好的,表达生动的,声音最大的,翻页最快的。

找出罗尼适合什么奖项着实费了我一番心思,我需要某种积极的东西,但确实没多少。我最后决定用"进步最快的"——相当牵强,但是我想,给他一个听起来美好的世界对他会有很大帮助的。

我颁给罗尼获奖证书和一本书——是那种在杂货店的收银台花49美分就能买一本的小金书。眼泪从他的面颊上滚落下来,把他脸上似乎永远存在的灰垢冲出了条纹,他把书紧紧抱在胸前,飘飘然地走回座位。我咽下了喉咙里上涌的硬块。

我这天的大部分时间都呆在班上,罗尼从未放下那本书,一次也没有。他爱不释手。

几天后,我回到那所学校访问。我注意到,罗尼在操场旁的长椅上,那本书摊开放在腿上。我看见他的嘴唇在动,像是在读给自己听。

罗尼的老师出现在我身边。"自从你送他那本书后,他从未把它放下

since you gave it to him.He wears it like a shirt,close to his heart.Did you know that's the first book he's ever actually owned?"

Fighting back tears,I approached Ronny and watched over his shoulder as his grimy finger moved slowly across the page.I placed my hand on his shoulder and asked, "Will you read me your book, Ronny?"He glanced up,squinted into the sun,and scooted over on the bench to make room for me.

And then,for the next few minutes,he read to me with more expression,clarity,and ease than I'd ever thought possible from him.The pages were already dog-eared,like the book had been read thousands of times already.

When he finished reading,Ronny closed his book,stroked the cover with his grubby hand and said with great satisfaction, "Good book."

A quiet pride settled over us as we sat on that playground bench, Ronny's hand now in mine.I at once wept and marveled at the young boy beside me.What a powerful contribution the author of that Little Golden Book had made in the life of a disadvantaged child.

At that moment,I knew I would get serious about my own writing career and do what that author had done,and probably still does—care enough to write a story that changes a child's life,care enough to make a difference.

I strive to be that author.

Judith A.Chance

过。他像穿衬衫那样带着它，把它贴在心口上。你知道那事实上是他拥有的第一本书吗？"

努力止住泪水，我走近罗尼，越过他肩膀看着他那脏兮兮的手指慢慢移过书页。我把手放在他肩上，问道："你能给我读读你的书吗，罗尼？"他抬头一瞥，被阳光刺得眯起了眼睛，迅速在长椅上移动为我腾出空位。

在之后的几分钟里，他读得远比我所预期的更生动、清晰而轻松。那书页已经卷了边，似乎这本书已经被读过上千次了。

读完后，罗尼合上书，用脏兮兮的小手敲敲封皮，以极大的满足之情说："一本好书。"

那时我们正坐在操场旁的长椅上，我握着罗尼的手，一种宁静的自豪之情在我们心中升腾。刹那间，我流泪了，我为身边的这个小男孩感到惊奇。那本小金书的作者为一个穷孩子的生活产生了多么巨大的影响啊！

那一刻，我懂得了要严肃地对待我自己的写作事业，做出那个作家曾做过的事情，也许依然能够做到——慎重地写一本能够改变孩子一生的书，慎重地施加影响。

我要力求成为那样的作家。

Cyberstepmother
网络继母

Only a mother knows a mother's fondness.

Lady Mary Wortley Montagu

只有一个作母亲的才能知道母亲强烈的爱。

玛丽·沃特莱·蒙塔古夫人

I've often felt that "stepparent",a label we attach to men and women who marry into families where children already exist,was coined merely for the simple reason that we need to call them something.It is most certainly an enormous "step",but one doesn't often feel as if the term"parent" truly applies.At least that's how I used to feel about being a stepmother to my husband's four children.

My husband and I had been together for six years,and with him I had watched as his young children became young teenagers.Although they lived primarily with their mother,they spent a lot of time with us.Over the years,we all learned to adjust,to become more comfortable with each other,and to adapt to our new family arrangement.We enjoyed vacations together,ate family meals,worked on homework, played baseball and rented videos.However,I continued to feel somewhat like an outsider,infringing upon foreign territory.There was a definite boundary line that could not be crossed,an inner family circle that excluded me.Since I had no children of my own,my experience of parenting was limited to my husband's four,and often I lamented that I would never know the special bond that exists between a parent and a child.

When the children moved to a town five hours away,my husband was understandably devastated.In order to maintain regular communication with the kids,we promptly set up an e-mail and chat-line service.This technology,combined with the telephone,would enable us to reach them on a daily basis by sending frequent notes and messages,and even chatting together when we were all on-line.

Ironically,these modern tools of communication can also be tools of alienation,making us feel out of touch and more in need of real human contact.If a computer message came addressed to "Dad",I'd feel forgotten and neglected.If my name appeared along with his,it

我总认为"继父母"这个词是我们给和一个已经有孩子的家庭建立婚姻关系的人贴上的标签,原因很简单:我们总是需要称呼他们什么。可以肯定这确实是人生中的非常重要的"一步",可我们却很少享受真正"父母"的待遇。至少我在做我丈夫4个孩子的后妈时曾经是这么认为的。

我和我的丈夫在一起已经6年了,我和他一起看着他的小孩子们成长为少年。虽然他们通常是和妈妈住的,但他们也和我们共度了很多时光。在这么多年中,我们都学会了调整自己,彼此和睦相处去适应新家庭氛围。我们一起度假,共享家庭聚餐,做家务,打垒球,看录像。可是在心里,我或多或少总是觉得我是一个闯入他人领地的外人。这个除我之外的家庭内部圈子,还是有一个很明显的不能越过的边界线。因为我没有自己的孩子,所以我作为家长的经验仅限于我丈夫的4个孩子,我经常伤心地觉得我永远不会感觉到家长和孩子之间存在的特殊的纽带关系。

当孩子们搬入离家5小时以外车程的镇子上时,我丈夫理所当然很牵挂。为了能和孩子们保持经常联系,我们装上了电脑,并且立即申请了电子邮件和在线聊天服务。这种技术,再加上电话,使我们能够通过经常发送信息来了解他们每天的生活,不仅如此,当我们都在线的时候,我们甚至可以在一起聊天。

具有讽刺意味的是,这种现代交流工具也可以疏远人们彼此之间的关系,让我们觉得很孤独,很需要真正的接触。如果一封来信写着"爸爸",我会觉得自己被遗忘、被忽视。如果我的名字和他一同出现,我就会一整

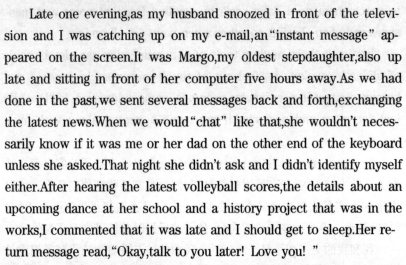

would brighten my day and make me feel like I was part of their family unit.Yet always there was some distance to be crossed,not just over the telephone wires.

Late one evening,as my husband snoozed in front of the television and I was catching up on my e-mail,an"instant message" appeared on the screen.It was Margo,my oldest stepdaughter,also up late and sitting in front of her computer five hours away.As we had done in the past,we sent several messages back and forth,exchanging the latest news.When we would"chat" like that,she wouldn't necessarily know if it was me or her dad on the other end of the keyboard unless she asked.That night she didn't ask and I didn't identify myself either.After hearing the latest volleyball scores,the details about an upcoming dance at her school and a history project that was in the works,I commented that it was late and I should get to sleep.Her return message read,"Okay,talk to you later! Love you! "

As I read this message,a wave of sadness ran through me and I realized that she must have thought she was writing to her father the whole time.She and I would never have openly exchanged such words of affection.Feeling guilty for not clarifying,yet not wanting to embarrass her,I simply responded,"Love you,too! Have a good sleep! "

I thought again of their family circle,that self-contained,private space where I was an intruder.I felt again the sharp ache of emptiness and "otherness".Then,just as my fingers reached for the keys to return the screen to black,Margo's final message appeared.It read, "Tell Dad good night for me,too."With tear-filled,blurry eyes,I turned the machine off.

Judy E.Carter

天都很快乐,让我觉得他们把我当成家庭的一员了。虽然距离仍然存在,而且不只像跨越空间距离一样那么简单。

一天夜里,我丈夫在电视机前打盹,我上网查看邮件,一条"即时信息"出现在屏幕上。是玛戈,我最大的继女,在5个小时以外的地方也在电脑前熬着夜。就像过去一样,我们在电脑前传递着信息,交流最近的新闻。每当我们这样聊天的时候,她不知道坐在另一端键盘前面的是谁——是我还是他爸爸,除非她问。那晚她没有问,我也没有表明。在谈论最近的排球比分,即将到来的校园舞会和书上的一个史学项目后,我建议说太晚了该休息了。她回复说:"好吧,以后再聊!爱你!"

当我读到这条信息时,一股悲伤的情绪涌上心头,我意识到,原来整个晚上她都认为她都在和她父亲说话!对我她是不会这样敞开心扉,这样充满感情的。带着没有澄清事实的犯罪感,而且也不想让她难堪,我只是回复到:"我也爱你!做个好梦!"

我再次想到了他们的家庭圈子,在这个只允许自己人享用的私人空间里我是一个闯入者。我又一次感觉到那种深切的痛苦,空虚寂寥,与他们格格不入。正当我伸出手准备关掉屏幕时,玛戈的最后一条信息来了:"替我和爸爸说晚安。"泪水浸湿了我的双眼,我关掉了电脑。

Writers in Prison
狱中作家

A moment's success pays for the failure of the years.

Robert Browning

十年寒窗无人问，一朝成名天下知。

罗伯特·伯朗宁

I was doing a guest writing workshop at Susanville State Prison near the Sierra Nevada foothills in northern California. Most of the men doing time there are sentenced to prison because of drugs. They are housed in huge dormitories in bunk beds. They have no privacy, no place to be alone, no place to think quietly. I had great apprehensions when I walked onto the prison grounds. I had taught writing workshops at many California prisons, but those prisons had cells. In cells, even if they are shared with another inmate, one can find at least a little writing time. Surely the men here at Susanville were not going to be interested in what I had to offer.

I had decided to spend my two days giving a monologue workshop. I wanted the men to have a chance to write and then perform before a camera. I wanted them to see themselves on video before I left the prison at the end of the second day. I felt that life in this prison had probably stripped them of most of their identity and that writing and performance art might restore some sense of who they were or who they could be.

I was pleased that twenty men had signed up for the class. This was the maximum number I had said I could take. I spent the first hour with them, talking about what it was like to be a writer. Telling them that there is a joy and a freedom in the words. That no matter how much they were all forced to be alike,dress alike,eat the same food,keep the same hours,that in their writing they could finally be different.As different as they wanted to be.

Writing,I told them,can be the most liberating of all the arts. You can be free with the word.There are no limits.I told them that every time I picked up a pencil or sat down at a computer or a typewriter that it was as if I was coming home,coming home to my art,my words,that this was a world that no one else could take away.This art

我那时在苏珊维尔州监狱开设写作客座讲习班。这个监狱靠近加州北部内华达山脉的丘陵地带。那里服刑的人大多因吸毒而入狱,他们的铺位被安置在很大的寝室里。他们没有私人空间,没有独处之处,也没有可以安静思考的地方。我怀着深深的忧虑踏上这块监狱的土地。我曾在加州许多监狱开设过写作讲习班,但那些监狱都有单间。即使是和别人共用,一个人至少可以找到一点点写作时间。毫无疑问,苏珊维尔监狱的人们不会对我的提议感兴趣的。

我决定用两天时间开一个独白写作讲座。我希望这些人能有机会写作,然后能够在摄像机前进行诵读表演。我希望在第二天结束课程和离开监狱之前,让他们在电视上看到他们自己。我感到,这个监狱里的生活也许已经剥夺了他们的大部分个性, 而写作和表演艺术也许能恢复一些关于他们是什么人、或者他们可以成为怎样的人的认识。

我感到高兴的是有20个人报名参加这个班。这是我的讲座能够承受的最多人数。第一个小时我和他们谈论成为作家是怎么回事。我告诉他们,在文字中有一种快乐和自由。我告诉他们,不论他们在多大程度上被迫彼此相似,穿着相似,饮食相同,作息一致,但是,在写作中他们最终可以彼此相异。他们想怎样不同就怎样不同。

我告诉他们, 写作也许是所有艺术中最解放的。你在文字中是自由的,那里没有界限。我告诉他们,每当我拿起笔,或者在电脑或者在打字机前坐下时,我总感觉像是回到了家,回到了我的艺术世界、话语之家,那是

生命的彩虹

would sustain me throughout all my days.

The men listened well and when I finally had them start their writing projects,they worked hard.There was only one,a young,very handsome blond man,who I worried about.He was reluctant to share during that first day when I had them writing their monologues.Every other student read and rewrote and read again,but this man sat quietly, erasing,writing,tearing up drafts,starting again.Whenever I would approach his desk,he quietly covered his paper with his arms.

"Can I see?"I would ask.

"It would be easier for me if you didn't,"he would answer and then a shy smile would appear.

I figured,what the heck.Even if he doesn't share his writing with the class,he's writing.He is choosing to spend his whole day in this hot,stuffy classroom working on something called a monologue.That morning he probably didn't even know the meaning of the word.This should make me happy.But it didn't.I was concerned about his need for privacy,about his inability to share,knowing that he didn't think his writing was good enough.

I had worked in prisons for too many years to be fooled by his shyness.I knew that many of the inmates had learned at a very young age that they could do nothing right.They had been abused and tormented as children and lacked any self-confidence.But no matter how much I praised the other prisoners he wouldn't relent. He went back to his dormitory that evening with his writing tucked into his jeans pocket.Many of the other men just left their work on the desks.Not him.He was taking no chance that I would read it after he was locked away behind the bars.He was right,of course.I would have made a beeline right for his desk the minute he got out the door.He had judged me right.

The second day all the men returned to the classroom.This was particularly pleasing to me.Even the young blond man.This was the day for reading and taping.I wondered how the silent,shy student would handle this.I was actually surprised to see him there.He had combed his long,blond hair and his shirt was neatly pressed.He had

一个任何人都无法夺走的世界。写作这门艺术支撑着我走过所有的日子。

这些人认真地聆听,当我最终要求他们开始他们自己的写作计划时,他们很努力。只有一个人,一个年轻的金发碧眼的英俊小伙子让我担心。第一天当我要求他们写独白时,他不情愿让别人看他的作品。其他每个学生都朗读、修改、再朗读,但他静静地坐着,擦除、再写、撕掉草稿、重新开始。无论何时我走近他的桌子,他总是用胳膊无声地遮住稿纸。

"我能看一看吗?"我问。

他会这样回答,"假如您不看,我会更轻松。"说着,脸上浮现出一种羞涩的微笑。

我思忖着,那有什么关系呢。即使他不在班上展示他的作品,他还是在写。他选择花一整天时间在这个闷热而不通气的教室里写某种叫做独白的东西,而那天早晨他可能连什么是独白都不知道。这本该让我高兴的,但是不。我关注的是他对于私人空间的需求,他不能向别人展示他的作品,我知道他是认为自己的作品不够好。

在监狱工作多年的经历使我不会被他的羞涩所欺骗。我知道许多囚犯都在很小的时候就认为自己一事无成。他们童年时饱受虐待和折磨,缺乏起码的自信心。然而无论我怎样称赞其他囚犯,都始终没有使这个小伙子变得随和。那天晚上回寝室时,他把自己的作品塞进牛仔裤口袋带走了。而其他许多人只是把自己的作品留在桌上。他没有。他不给我任何机会,担心我会在他被锁在铁栅栏后偷看他的作品。当然,他是对的。他一走出教室,我就会径直走向他的桌子。他正确地评判了我。

第二天所有学生都回到了教室。这让我特别高兴。连那个金发碧眼的年轻人也来了。这天我们要朗读和打字。我很想知道这个安静、羞涩的学生将怎办。实际上,我对再次见到他就感到很惊讶了。他梳理了长长的金发,穿上了熨得很伏贴的衬衫。显然,他考虑到将要上镜,并且希望让大

obviously thought about the fact that he was going to be filmed and wanted to look his best.At last I was going to hear what he wrote.

He didn't say much during the performances.I had given the men fairly loose instructions about who should be speaking in their monologues.I had,though,told them that I wanted to hear their characters tell me what it is they really wanted,what it was that no one understood about them,and why they needed to talk. He sat there quietly, watching the work of his fellow inmates.One of the men had written a monologue for God,and another had been Abraham Lincoln,another Martin Luther King,Jr. Some of the monologues were funny,others serious.Even though they hadn't had time to memorize their lines,once they began reading,the scripts in their hands were hardly noticeable, and I was extremely moved by their work.

Finally,he was the only one who hadn't read his monologue. When all the others were finished I asked him,"Are you ready now?"

"I don't think so,"he answered in such a gentle voice.

Then the men were on him.

"Man,if I can do it,you can do it.Try it.You'll like it.Come on man,don't be shy.Nobody's going to judge you here."

So he got up,took his script to the performance area and stood before the camera.He looked so young.The papers in his hands were shaking like frightened birds,but he looked with determination into the eye of the camera and opened up his monologue.

"My name is Bruce.I am twenty-one years old and I am dead.I am dead because I spent time in prison for drugs and I didn't care.I didn't care about me.I went to bed every night just counting the days 'till I could get out and get that next fix.I would kill for my next fix.I would die for my next fix."

He went on about his life,how he was raised in poverty by alcoholic parents,beaten,hungry,no life at all,shuffled back and forth through foster homes.While he read,he showed scars on his body,the burn marks on his arms where a drunken father had extinguished cigarettes,the cuts on his wrists where he had tried to take his own life.I couldn't help it.The tears began forming in my eyes,hot and

家看到他最好的一面。我终于可以听到他写了什么了。

在别人表演过程中他少言寡语。我曾就谁在独白给予他们相当宽泛的指导。不过,我告诉他们,我希望听到他们独白中的人物告诉我他们真正渴望什么,告诉我他们不为人知的一面,以及他们为什么需要陈述。他静静地坐在那里,观看同伴们的表演。有个人写的是上帝的独白,另一个人写的是亚伯拉罕·林肯,还有个人写的是小马丁·路德·金。有些独白有趣,另一些严肃。虽然他们没有时间背诵台词,但是一旦开始朗诵,他们手中的剧本就几乎不引人注意,而我却被他们的作品深深地打动了。

最后,他是唯一没有朗诵独白的人。其他人都演完后,我问他:"现在你准备好了吗?"

"我想没有。"他轻声回答。

这时其他人给他鼓劲:

"伙计,既然我能做到,你也就能做到。尝试一下吧,你会喜欢的。来吧伙计,别害羞。这儿没人要评判你。"

于是他站起来,拿着他的剧本走到表演区,站在摄像机前。他看上去非常年轻。尽管手中的稿纸抖得像受惊的鸟,他还是坚定地看着摄像头,开始了独白。

"我叫布鲁斯,21岁,已死去。我死了,因为我由于吸毒在监狱中度日却并不在乎。我不关心自己。我每天晚上睡觉前都数着日子,直到我出来的一天,那时我要再打一针。我会为我的下一针毒品去杀人。我会为我的下一针毒品去杀人的。"

他继续讲述他的生活,他怎样在贫困中由酗酒的父母养大,挨打,受饥,生活凄惨,在寄养家庭间来回周转。他一边读,一边给我们看身上的伤疤,他那喝醉酒的父亲在他胳膊上按熄烟头留下的烫伤,他试图自杀在手腕上留下的割伤。我情难自禁,灼热而痛苦的泪盈满眼眶。天哪,我为什么

painful.My God,why had I asked him to share this horrible pain?Then he got to the end of his story.

"Even though I died right there in prison,I want to tell you something.The reason I need to talk to you today.I have risen again, just like in the Bible.I am reborn.One day a woman came in and told me to write.And I had never written before,but I did it anyway.I sat for eight hours in a chair and focused the way I have never focused before.I could never even sit still before! I wrote out my ugly life,and then I was able to finally feel something.To feel pity.For myself.When no one else was ever able to feel it.And I felt something else.I felt joy.I was writing,and what I was writing was good.I was a writer! And I was going to get up in front of all those men in that class,and I would say that this..."At these words he held up his little manuscript. "This is more important to me than any drug.What I wanted to tell you was that I died a drug addict,and I was reborn as a writer."

We all sat there stunned.The camera kept running.He took a self-conscious little bow.Then he said,"Thank you,"once again in his quiet voice.And then the men broke out in spontaneous applause.He walked over to me and took my hands.Inmates are not allowed to touch their teachers,but I let him anyway."You have given me something,"he said,"that no drug has ever given me.My self-respect."

I think of him often.I pray that he has continued to find respect for himself through the written word.I know,though,that that day in that room with those men,a writer was born.After a long and terrible journey,a lost soul had come home,home to the words.

Claire Braz-Valentine

要他讲述如此可怕的痛苦？这时他说完了故事。

"尽管我就在这儿，在监狱里死去了，我还是想告诉你们一些东西。那就是我今天需要告诉你们这一切的原因。我复活了，正如在圣经中那样。我获得了新生。有一天，一位女士走进来，让我写作。我以前从未写过，但无论如何我做到了。我坐了8个小时冷板凳，以一种我从未试过的方式聚精会神地写作。而我以前甚至不能安静地坐下来！我写出了我丑陋的生活，然后我终于能感受到某种东西。我感到怜悯。当其他人都无动于衷时，我对我自己感到怜悯。我还有另一种感受。我感到高兴。我在写作，而且写得不错。我是一个作家！我将在班上那些同学面前站起来，我会告诉他们这个……"说着，他举起薄薄的手稿，"这对我而言比任何毒品都更重要。我想告诉你们的是:我以一个吸毒成瘾的人的身份死去，却以一个作家的身份重生。"

我们都坐在那儿，目瞪口呆。只有摄像机还在继续拍摄。他自觉地微微鞠了一躬，然后再次以平静的声调说:"谢谢。"这时人们自发地爆发出热烈掌声。他走近我，和我握手。囚犯是不允许接触老师的，可无论如何，我让他那么做了。"您给了我某种东西,"他说,"那是任何毒品都不曾给我的。我的自尊。"

我常常想起他。我为他祈祷,祝愿他继续从写下的文字中找到自尊。不管怎样,我知道,那天,在那个屋子里,在那些人的见证下,一位作家诞生了。经历了一段漫长而可怕的旅程后,一颗迷失的心灵终于回家了,回到了话语之家。

Happy Holidays
节日快乐

In prison, holidays are the worst. Birthdays, anniversaries, Thanksgiving, Christmas, even Valentine's Day can be a "bummer." It's difficult and painful to be away from those we love-to be left out of the celebrations and the memory making. Many times, we feel a little forgotten or overlooked.

Birthdays in prison come and go without the comfort of cake with candles and the magic of blowing them out. Christmas mornings are without a fancy tree or presents. Thanksgivings are hard to feel thankful for, with dinner served on a cold, metal cafeteria tray.

My first Thanksgiving in prison, I refused to eat. My first birthday I spent alternating between rage and feeling more sorry for myself than ever before. On Christmas, I wouldn't even get out of bed. I stayed under the covers to hide the tears I cried all day.

So holidays in here are the worst-at least I thought hey were until I realized a few things. Once I stripped away all the commercialism and hype, I saw what holidays were all about. They're elaborate excuses we use to take a look at our lives, our successes and failures, and to spend quality time with our loved ones.

In here or out there, we can still take stock of ourselves and make plans, dream dreams, examine our behavior to see what we like and don't like. Even in here, we have the power to change what falls short of our ideal self image.

Not being able to spend quality time with those we love is a little tougher-until we realize that the people we care for are always with us-in our hearts and minds. And just as they're with us, we are with them in spirit.

The days we can't spend together physically,we can still take time to remember them fondly... Making phone calls,sending cards or letters helps both us and our loved ones.

在监狱里,过节是一种煎熬。生日,周年纪念,感恩节,圣诞节,甚至情人节都会令人郁闷至极。因为远离我们所爱的人,不能和他们一起庆祝各种节日,不能和他们一起制造将来的回忆,让人觉得难熬,痛苦万分。很多时候,我们会有一丝被遗忘或被忽视的感觉。

狱中的生日没有点燃蜡烛的生日蛋糕的慰藉,没有吹灭蜡烛那一瞬间的魔力,就这么来了又走了,圣诞节的早晨也没有别致的圣诞树和小礼物,面对着盛在冰冷的金属自助餐盘中的晚餐,我们也很难在感恩节对什么产生感激之情。

在狱中过第一个感恩节的时候,我拒绝吃任何东西。第一个狱中的生日,是在暴怒和自怜两种情绪中交替度过的。而圣诞那天,我甚至都没有起床,躲在被窝里哭了一整天。

所以,在监狱里过节是一种煎熬,至少我是这么认为的,直到后来我明白了一些事情才改变了我的想法。在褪去所有关于节日的商业用语和天花乱坠的宣传之后,我懂得了节日到底是什么。节日就是我们精心编造的一些借口,我们借口过节来审视我们的生活,审视我们的成功和失败,并且借口过节来和我们所爱的人度过一段美好的节日时光。

无论是在狱中还是狱外,我们仍然能掂量自己的能力并且制订计划,勾勒梦想,检查我们的行为,以此来发现我们喜欢什么,不喜欢什么。哪怕在监狱里,我们也有力量来改变那些损坏我们自身理想形象的东西。

不能和我们所爱的人一起度过美好时光让人感到有点难过,直到后来我们明白了,我们关心的人一直和我们在一起,在我们的心里,在我们的脑海里。正因为我们是在一起的,所以我们精神上与他们同在。

虽然我们不能一起度过那些节日,但是我们可以给我们所爱的人打电话,寄卡片,或者写信,仍然可以深深地记住他们……

其他人不会让我们感到快乐。特别的地点和特别的人可能会使我们

Other people don't make us happy.Special places and people might help the mood,but the celebration and love comes from within. The challenge is to find it there-a state of mind,a positive attitude.It's easy to use a holiday as an excuse to be sad or edgy.I've been there. Our challenge is to celebrate every day as special.Life is a precious gift,whether we're in jail or not.

I'm planning a celebration every day this year-a celebration of life.You're invited.Happy Holidays! RSVP.

Daryl D.Foley

心情愉快,但是欢庆和爱是发自内心的。在监狱里想要找到这两样东西会是一个挑战,那就是愉快的心情和积极的态度。我们很容易以过节为借口而感到悲伤或者烦躁, 所以我们的挑战就是把每一天都要当做特别的日子来庆祝。生命是一件珍贵的礼物,无论我们是身陷囹圄还是快乐自由。

我正在计划庆祝今年的每一天, 庆祝生命。我邀请你来和我一起庆祝。节日快乐!

期待您的回信。

Writing from the Heart
用心写作

When you write from the heart, you not only light the dark path of your readers, you light your own way as well.

Marjorie Holmes

当你用心写作时，你不仅照亮了你的读者黑暗的道路，也照亮了你自己的道路。

马乔里·福尔摩斯

I was pulling together materials for the first night of my Advanced Writing for Publication class when I was interrupted by a confident, demanding voice.

"Are you Bud Gardner?"

The man standing in the doorway to my office stood about 5 feet 8, weighed about 125 pounds, and was all business.

"Yes, I'm Bud. Have a seat. How may I help you?"

"I'm Joe Howard. I came by to meet you, to decide if I want to

我正在为我的高级出版写作班的第一晚的课程集中组织材料，突然，一个自信的命令式的声音打断了我的思路。

"你是巴德·加德纳吗？"

说话的人站在我的办公室门口，他西装革履，大约5英尺8英寸高，125磅左右。

"是的，我就是巴德。请坐。有事吗？"

"我是乔·霍华德。我顺路来见见你，以便决定我是否需要参加你今晚开始上课的班。你知道，我已经60多岁了，没有多少时间可以浪费，连一分

take your class beginning tonight.You see,I'm over sixty,and I don't have enough time left to waste even a minute of it."

Joe Howard,I learned,was a retired,veteran reporter for the *Los Angeles Times*, now living in my home town.

"I still do a little stringing for the *Times* now and then.I covered Ross Perot when he came to town a while back."

"With your background as a seasoned journalist,why on earth would you want to take this class?"I asked.

"Because I'm looking for a change.I've spent most of my life writing hard news stuff.I want to look at other types of writing.I know I have a couple of books in me.Maybe some fiction,too."His eyes narrowed."The question is,what have you got to offer me?"

"In this advanced class,we begin by reviewing how to sell articles to magazines."

"Been there,done that,"he snapped."What else?"

"We'll study how to get a nonfiction book published—either by sending out a book proposal to a trade publication or by self-publishing."

"What?"he scolded."Self-publishing? Isn't that for amateurs who can't interest major publishers?"

"Not really.Self-publishing allows a writer to get a great idea to the marketplace first,to control the book project from start to finish, to become a publisher.Three of my former students have become millionaires because they chose to self-publish.One author,Jane Nelsen,has self-published fourteen books,which nets her one million dollars a year from her writing and speaking engagements."

"Phfffftt! Not for me,"he said,irritated."What else?"

"We'll take a look at the short story structure,and many students will want to begin working on a novel."

"Oh really,"he said cynically. "Just how many novels have your students turned out anyway?"

"I'm not sure.Nancy Elliott,Bettina Flores,Naida West,Jim Dearing, Ethel Bangert,and many other fine authors have turned out novels

钟也不行。"

乔·霍华德,我知道这个名字,他是《洛杉矶时代》的一个已经退休的经验丰富的记者,现住在我的家乡小镇。

"我现在偶尔还为《洛杉矶时代》做一点特约记者。前不久罗斯·佩洛特来到镇上,我负责报道全程。"

"你有作为一个经验丰富的新闻记者的背景,到底为何还想参加这个班呢?"我问道。

"因为我在寻求一种改变。我已经花了大半生时间写实实在在的新闻材料。我想尝试其他风格的写作。我知道我正在构思两本书。也许还包括小说。"他眯起眼睛。"问题是,你将提供给我什么?"

"在这个高级写作班,我们一开始讲评怎样让稿子在杂志上发表。"

"这我已经做到了,"他厉声地说。"还有什么?"

"我们将研究怎样使一本非小说类的书出版——通过向商业出版社提出图书出版计划或者自主出版。"

"什么?"他斥责道。"自主出版?那不是为那些主要出版商不感兴趣的业余作家准备的吗?"

"并非如此。自主出版首先使得作者能够对市场情况有个大致概念,自始至终掌控出书计划,甚至成为一个出版商。我从前的3个学生由于选择自主出版已经成为百万富翁。作家简·内尔森已经自主出版了14本书,这使得她通过写作和做报告每年净赚一百万美元。"

"哼?!那不适合我,"他恼怒地说。"还有什么?"

"我们将注视短篇小说的结构,而许多学生都想开始写小说。"

"哦,真的吗,"他挖苦地说。"那究竟你的学生写出多少篇小说了?"

"我不能确定。南希·埃利奥特,贝蒂纳·弗洛里斯,奈达·韦斯特,吉姆·迪林,埃塞尔·班戈特,以及其他很多好作者都在参加我们的写作班后,写出了自己的小说。"

since taking classes in our writing program."

"Anything else?"he said,unimpressed.

"The whole purpose of this advanced class is to step up production,to turn out more articles,make multiple sales from one idea,to sell to the global market,and to get books published."

"You can do all of that in one semester?"he growled.

"Oh yes,we'll get some articles in print this semester,but the class will be long over before any books appear.That's okay. Knowing how the publishing industry works and having step-by-step processes to follow—that's what this class is all about."

"Is that it?"he said,beginning to tune out.

"We'll also talk about how to run an efficient home office,how to use the five energy levels we experience each day to turn out our best writing,and how to handle rejection,procrastination and writer's block."

"Writer's block?Give me a break.No serious writer ever gets blocked."

Wow! What an irascible,old curmudgeon, I thought.If he took the class,I knew I was in for it.He'd constantly challenge me on every concept I presented and would make life miserable for me.I'd had enough and decided to get rid of him.

"Then I guess the class isn't for you,"I said firmly.

"I'll decide that,"he snapped. "What kind of writing do you see me doing?"

As I looked deep into his eyes,for the first time I saw the pain he was feeling.I had nothing to lose.

"Why don't you try your hand at poetry?"I said softly.

"What?Poetry?Me?For God's sake,why?"his voice rising.

"It just might help you get in touch with your true feelings."

That stopped him cold.He sat there staring at me.It was a long time before he spoke.

"I've never thought about writing poetry.I'm not sure I want to reveal my feelings in print,"he said,no longer fighting.

"还有什么吗？"他对我的话无动于衷,淡淡地问道。

"这个高级写作班的全部宗旨在于提升作品,写出更多的文章,用一个想法进行多重销售,把作品销售到全球市场,以及使书得以出版。"

"你能在一学期内做到所有这些？"他用低沉而愤怒的声音说。

"哦,是的,我们这学期要发表几篇文章,但是课程会早在任何书出版之前结束。这没问题。了解出版业是怎样运营的及其按部就班的实现过程,以便追随它——这就是这门课所涉及的全部内容。"

"就这些？"他说,思想开始走神。

"我们还将谈谈如何经营一个高效的家庭办公室,如何使用我们每天经历的5种精力水平,以便写出最好的作品,如何处理退稿、拖稿,以及如何处理作家思路的阻塞。"

"作家思路的阻塞？打断一下,严肃认真的作家是不会思路阻塞的。"

哇！一个多么暴躁的坏脾气老头,我想道。如果他来上课,我知道自己就惨了。他会在我提出的每个概念上不断地向我挑战,使我的生活苦不堪言。我已经受够了,于是决定摆脱他。

"我觉得这门课不适合你,"我肯定地说。

"我自己会决定,"他发怒了。"你看我适合写哪类作品？"

当我深深地望着他的眼睛时,我第一次发现了他所感受的痛苦。我没有看错。

"为什么你不试试写诗？"我柔和地说。

"什么？诗？我？务必讲清楚,为什么？"他提高声音说。

"也许这恰恰能够帮助你了解自己的真实情感。"

这句话让他愣住了。他坐在那儿瞪着我。过了很长一段时间才开口说话。

"我从未想过写诗。我不确定我是否愿意把我的感受公开发表,"他说道,不再和我争辩。

"I understand."It was time to bring this to an end. "Look,why don't you come to the first session tonight,then make up your mind about taking the class.Okay?"

As he walked down the hall,he stopped and stared back at me for a full minute.Then he was gone.I thought I'd seen the last of him. *Good riddance*, I thought.But I was wrong.He not only showed up but sat through the full three-hour class,then asked to see me after class.

"Okay,you're on.I'll write you three poems a week.Deal?"

"Deal,"I said,trying to act confident,my stomach churning.

Joe Howard was true to his word.The next week,the week following,and every week after that he turned in three poems for me to critique.At first they were rather stiff and formal but carried great energy and power.Then as the weeks wore on,I began to see a softness appear in his poems.

I wish I hadn't agreed so quickly to Joe's deal of turning in three poems each week.Why?Because he turned in three poems to me each week—for five years.I couldn't get rid of the guy.He joined a poetry group in town and read his poems in public readings.He even read some of them on radio.Eventually,he produced a play of his best poems that was presented one weekend in our campus theater, featuring some professional actors and readers.

As students read their work aloud during the class,Joe pulled no punches in critiquing them.He always gave good,solid advice—even if it was harsh at times.Students respected and admired him,but didn't dare challenge his authority.

Then one night during the second year,he asked to read a poem to the class.I was taken aback.He'd never asked to read aloud before. The poem he read was about a conflict he'd had with his daughter.As he began reading it,he was confident,self-assured.About a third of the way into the poem,he burst into tears.The students and I were shocked.This old curmudgeon was actually crying.

I didn't know what to say.In thirty years of teaching,I'd never faced a situation like this.I decided to wait.

Joe got under control and began to read again.He broke into

"我理解。"是该结束这一切的时候了。"你看,你可以今晚先来听听第一堂课,然后再决定是否上这门课。行吗?"

当他走出大厅时,他停下回头盯着我足足看了一分钟,然后才走。我以为这是最后一次见他。摆脱掉他最好,我想。但是我错了。他不仅来上课,而且整整3个小时的课都坐在那里,课后还要求见我。

"好吧,你赢了。我会每周写3首诗给你。成交?"

"成交,"我说,努力表现出自信,而我的胃里在翻腾。

乔·霍华德是信守诺言的。第二周、第三周、以及之后的每一周,他都交3首诗给我,让我评论。开始这些诗是僵化而刻板的,但却带有巨大的能量和力量。随着一周周过去,我逐渐开始发现他的诗显现出温柔。

我宁愿我不曾这么爽快地同意乔,让他每周交我3首诗。为什么?因为他每周都交给我3首诗——这样持续了5年。我无法摆脱这个家伙。他参加了镇上的一个诗歌团体,并在公开朗读会上读他自己写的诗。他甚至在广播上朗读他的一些诗。最后,他写了一部由他的最佳诗作构成的诗剧,并请到一些专业演员和朗诵者在一个周末到我们校园的剧院上演。

当学生在课堂上大声朗诵他们的诗作时,他总是毫不留情地批评他们。他总给予好的、慎重的建议——虽然有时是严厉的。学生们都尊敬并钦佩他,而从不敢挑战他的权威。

第二年上这门课的一个晚上,乔要求在班上朗诵一首诗。我大吃一惊。他以前从未要求大声朗读作品呀。他朗读的诗是关于他和女儿之间的一次冲突。朗诵开始时,他沉着而自信。大约读到诗的三分之一时,他突然哭了出来。我和其他学生都震惊了。这个衰老的坏脾气老头的确在哭。

我不知该说什么。我在30年的教学生涯中从未碰见这种情形。我决定等待。

乔控制住情绪,再次开始朗读。他又一次止不住哭泣而中断朗读。我

tears a second time.Again I waited,not knowing what to do.

Embarrassed,fighting for control,he read again...cried...stopped... read again...then finished the poem,weeping.

The room was deadly quiet.I waited what seemed like an eternity.Then I finally spoke.

"Thanks for sharing,Joe,"I said quietly.

Emotionally moved,the class exploded into applause. Everyone was cheering,smiling,and wiping tears away.

"Hold it! "shouted Joe,now back in control. "I've got something to say."Then he told how he had interviewed me before the first class a year and a half ago and how much he had enjoyed the class and writing poetry.

"When Bud first asked me to write poetry,I couldn't believe it.It was difficult at first because I couldn't get in touch with myself.Then as the months passed by,I began to go below the layers of the crusty reporter I'd been to the core me.What you heard and saw tonight with this poem came from the real Joe Howard.I finally got in touch with my true feelings."His eyes filled with tears again. "Thank you for sharing this moment with me."

Triggered by this experience with Joe,I created and have delivered a speech all over the western United States and Alaska titled "Writing from the Heart",which opens with Joe's story.And to show the brilliance of his great talent,during that speech I read the following poem:

"The Black Stallion"
by Joe Howard

He was wild and free.
Small,muscular,hoofed.

Ranged far and wide.

Knew no boundaries.

又一次等待着,不知道该做些什么。

乔感到困窘,于是竭力控制住自己,并再次开始朗读……哭泣……中断……再朗读……最后终于流着泪把诗读完了。

教室里极度安静。我等候了似乎永恒的一段时间。最后我终于开口。

"谢谢分享,乔,"我轻声地说。

班上的同学们被深深地感动了,班里爆发出掌声。每个人都在欢呼,微笑,拭去眼泪。

"静一下!"乔大声说,现在他已经恢复了自制。"我有些话要说。"然后他告诉我们,他怎样在一年半前开课之前会见我,以及他多么喜欢全班,多么喜欢诗歌创作。

"当巴德第一次要求我去写诗时,我不敢相信这一点。万事开头难,因为我不能触及到我自己的内心。随着一个月一个月时光的流逝,我的心开始穿透新闻记者的硬壳,回到内部的真我。你们今晚从这首诗中所见所闻的东西是出自真正的乔·霍华德。我终于能触及我的真实情感。"他的眼眶里再次充满了泪水。"谢谢你们和我共享这一时刻。"

受到乔的经历的启发,我创作了题为"用心写作"的演讲,在整个美国西部和阿拉斯加演说,而这个演讲就以乔的故事开头。为了展示乔出众的才华,我在演讲中会朗诵他写的如下这首诗:

黑色牡马

乔·霍华德

他狂野,自由,

年少,健壮,

踢踏着四处游荡。

他无拘无束,

除了饥饿,

Except those of hunger,
fatigue,disease.

Wild he was.
Strong he was.
Free he was.
Fearless he was.

Till they trapped him.
Threw him off his feet.
Tied his legs.
Dropped a tarp over him.
Beat the fight out of him.

Then they pulled the tarp off.
Burned him with their brand.
Took the bindings from his legs.
Jerked him back upright.
Saddled him,rode him,
fed him,drove him.
Until the memory
of what he'd been
was lost in the pain.

Time passed.
And he grew old.
Grey.Spindly.
No longer usable.
Worthless to them.
Feed cost.

疲劳和疾病。

他如此野性，
如此强壮，
如此自由，
如此无畏。

直到他们捕获了他，
掀翻他的脚，
拴起他的腿，
给他盖上油布，
毒打到他不再反抗。

然后他们把油布拿开，
在他身上烙下印记。
解开腿上的捆绑，
猛地拉他背朝上，
装上马鞍，骑到他身上，
喂养他，驱赶他，
直到那关于他
曾是怎样的回忆，
在痛苦中淡去。

时光飞逝，
他变老了。
衰老，瘦弱，
不再有用。
他对他们失去了价值，
喂养成为破费。
于是他们把它带回去，

So they took him back,
To where they'd found him.
Cast him out.
On old ground.
To face what was now strange.

Alone,he stood...For a while.
Alone,he did not move...For a while.
Then,deep within,memory stirred.
And his head lifted.

His eye caught sight of sky.
Of peak.Of wild others.
And he bent to feed,
not yet dead.
Rose to see,not yet down.
Moved to explore,not yet lame.

Life returned...Slowly...Slowly.
Healing began...Gently...Gently.
And the old black stallion
heard his heart beat...once more.

The old black stallion found his
soul...once more.
Knew he was alive...once more.
Knew he was free...once more.
Knew he was home...once more.

Like the black stallion,all writers at times despair,but if they will

到那曾发现他的地方。
把他放逐
在古老的土地上，
面对现在是陌生的一切。

孤独地，他站在那里……好一会，
孤独地，他一动不动……好一会，
此时，他内心深处，回忆澎湃，
他抬起了头。

他的眼睛仰望天空，
投向山峰，望着野生的他物，
他想低头去吃草，
只要还没有死去。
他奋起去看，趁着还没有倒下，
他移动着去探测，趁着尚未残废。

生命回归了……慢慢地……慢慢地，
伤口开始愈合……逐渐地……逐渐地，
而这匹年老的黑色牡马，
再一次地……听到了他自己的心跳。

年老的黑色公马找到了他的
灵魂……再一次地，
知道自己还活着……再一次地，
知道自己是自由的……再一次地，
知道他回家了……再一次地。

　　正如这匹黑色公马一样，所有的作家都会有沮丧的时候，但只要他们
发掘他们自身更深层次的东西，他们也能找到恢复力来推动自己，去达到

dig deeper within themselves,they,too,will find the resilience to push on,to reach their goals.

I learned from Joe Howard,my dear friend and seasoned writer, that we must always write from the heart,and not just from the head. When we write stories from the heart,we connect with readers on a deeper level as we guide them to new levels of thinking,feeling, seeing,perceiving,and being.In short,we allow them to change.As writers we must see ourselves as change agents,but not manipulators, who—through heartfelt stories—offer readers changes of thought patterns that can inform,entertain,or persuade them with new ideas.

Thank you Joe Howard,my good friend.I'm a better person,writer, teacher and speaker because you passed my way.

Bud Gardner

他们的目标。

我从乔·霍华德——我亲爱的朋友和经验丰富的作家身上学到,我们必须始终写心中感受到的东西,而不能仅仅写头脑所想的东西。当我们用心去写故事时,我们就会在更深的层次上和读者的心联系在一起,引领他们到达更高的思考、感受、观察和感知存在的水平。简而言之,我们允许他们改变。身为作家的我们必须把自己看做改变的代理人,而不是操纵者。作家通过写出真诚的发自内心的故事来为读者提供能够告知的、娱乐的或用新思想劝说的思维模式的变化。

谢谢你,乔·霍华德,我的好朋友。由于你经过我的生命之旅,我才成为一个更好的人——作家、教师和演讲者。

Pegasus's Wings
珀加索斯的翅膀

Each handicap is like a hurdle in a steeplechase, and when you ride up to it, if you throw your heart over,the horse will go along,too.

Lawrence Bixby

每一个障碍就像障碍赛中的一个跨栏，当你跑向它时,如果你身心投入,倾力而为,那马也会一同跨越障碍。

劳伦斯·彼克斯比

I've always loved horses,and for some time I'd been looking for a volunteer opportunity in my new community.The idea that I might be able to pursue both interests at once hadn't actually crossed my mind.So I couldn't get to the phone fast enough when I saw an ad in the paper about a search for volunteers at a therapeutic riding center for handicapped children.

"Yes,we're still looking for people,"the woman told me. "We're having a training session for new volunteers this Saturday.You're welcome to come."

我一直都很喜欢马，有段时间我也试图在新搬去的社区中寻找机会当志愿者。我从没有想到过会有一个机会可以让我的两种兴趣得到完美的结合，所以当我在报纸上看到一所专为残障儿童开办的马术治疗中心要招聘志愿者的广告的时候，我简直迫不及待地就冲到电话前。

"是的,我们还在招聘中。"那个女士告诉我,"我们这个星期六有一个专门针对新志愿者的培训。欢迎你来参加。"

"Thanks,"I answered,barely containing my enthusiasm. "I'll be there."

I joined a small group of new volunteers that day.We were perfect strangers with an instant connection,all drawn there by the same potent mix of heart and soul—a passion for helping,a passion for horses,and a simple knowing that we had come to the right place.By the end of the training session,we all knew we'd be back for the first of many weekly riding classes together.

That first Saturday,ten children between the ages of eight and twelve showed up.Ten struggling young bodies and ten eager,loving smiles greeted us."This is Robbie,"said the instructor,placing a gentle hand on each small shoulder as she conducted a round of introductions. "And this is Christine."We went around the circle of excited faces.All the children faced some level of physical or mental challenge—sometimes both.Jenny had multiple sclerosis,Kevin lived with cerebral palsy,Christine with Down's syndrome,and Robbie a spinal-cord injury.I marveled at these children,healthy souls and wholesome appetites for living shining through their bodily constraints.

The following Saturday,I arrived at the stables in time to groom my assigned horse before class,put on his tack and ensure that he was sound,calm and ready for his small rider.This week,I would be handling Stripe,a speckled-gray Appaloosa with comfortably rounded sides and an indulgent,ever-patient nature.

Today,Stripe was the designated therapy horse for nine-year-old Katie,a victim of muscular dystrophy.

Curly auburn hair framing her delicate,pale face,Katie arrived at the stables in a wheelchair.The spokes glistened in the sun as her mother helped her up,steadied her and introduced us.My eyes met Katie's—an exchange full of shared excitement and anticipation. "Katie has been waiting impatiently for hours,"her mother explained with a smile.

We set about preparing for the ride.I fitted and attached Katie's safety helmet and adjusted Stripe's specially adapted saddlery.I

"谢谢,我会来参加的。"我答道,简直抑制不住喜悦之情。

那天我加入了一个由新志愿者组成的小组,我们谁也不认识谁,可是却一见如故。我们来到这里出于同样的原因,那就是我们全心全意想要帮助残障儿童,而且对马也有无比深厚的感情,并且我们很清楚地知道我们来对了地方。在培训结束时,我们都知道,自己会再回来,开始教授每周一次的骑马课程。

第一个星期六,治疗中心来了10个8~12岁的小孩子。这10个身体有残障的孩子兴致勃勃地向我们打招呼,10张可爱的笑脸充满了渴望。"这是小罗比,这是小克里斯汀,"教练一边介绍他们的名字一边用手轻轻地拍着他们的娇小肩膀。我们慢慢地扫视了一圈,他们的小脸蛋一个个激动无比。这些孩子都面临着身体上或者智力上不同程度的障碍,有的孩子甚至有双重障碍。珍妮患有多发性硬化症,凯文患有大脑麻痹症,克里斯汀有先天痴呆,而罗比的脊椎神经受了伤。看到他们我感到非常惊讶,在身体缺陷的束缚下他们健康的心灵和对美好生活的向往依然闪耀着动人的光芒。

第二个星期六,我在上课前及时赶到马厩来照料分配给我的那匹马,我为马儿上好鞍,确保他状态良好,精神稳定,能以不错的状态来迎接他的小骑士。这个星期我负责的马儿名叫"条纹",一匹身上有斑点的灰色阿帕卢萨马,他有着舒适的圆形的侧腹,天性宽容而且有耐心。

今天"条纹"被指定给9岁的患有肌肉萎缩症的凯蒂做治疗。

小凯蒂坐着轮椅来到了马厩,赭色的卷发搭在她苍白娇弱的小脸上。凯蒂的妈妈扶她起来站稳,然后向凯蒂介绍了我们,轮椅的轮辐在阳光下闪闪发光。我和凯蒂目光相碰,我觉察到她的眼里充满了激动和期待,和我一样。"凯蒂等了几个小时,都有点不耐烦了",她妈妈微笑地解释道。

我们开始做骑马的准备。我调整好凯蒂的安全帽,给她戴上、系好,并且调整了一下"条纹"的专用马具。我帮助凯蒂上马,把她在马鞍里安顿

helped her mount and shared her triumphant grin as she settled into the saddle,perched above and beyond her limitations.I led Stripe around the arena during the class,quietly coaching both horse and rider as the instructor led the group from the center of the ring.We walked,trotted and moved together for an hour.Katie's tortured body gradually relaxed into Stripe's fluid movements,becoming one with the animal.

In silent awe,I let the wordless,poignant communication between Katie and Stripe unfold.Acutely sensitive to her well-being,Stripe intuitively softened his gait at the slightest perception of Katie's imbalance or discomfort in the saddle.The tone of her voice induced the same effect,even though she was unable to use verbal commands that the horse was trained to recognize.Surprise,delight,hesitation,fear— Stripe understood and responded patiently,lovingly—like a great teacher.

At the end of the class,I helped Katie dismount.Color in her cheeks now,she smiled radiantly and arched her thin arms around Stripe's lowered neck.He kept his head down.Burying her face in his mane,Katie murmured softly, "I love you,Stripe."I stood motionless a few feet away,touched by a moment of uncommon beauty.

The magic drew me back each week.No two Saturdays were the same.Rotations of therapy horses and riders gave volunteers the opportunity to get to know each animal and child.Every Saturday offered a glimpse of an intensely intimate connection between equine and human spirit.Every Saturday revealed the power of this fabled four-legged creature to triumph over a child's physical and mental adversity.Every Saturday,a child held the reins of freedom and borrowed Pegasus's wings.

For me,volunteering was a personal journey into unexpected enrichment and inspiration.I helped small children revel in another realm of physical and spiritual being,a space only their horses could create for them.I saw these children empowered and renewed by their equine companions.I rediscovered my deep love for horses and drew lessons from their gentle ways.And last but not least,I learned

好,她栖息在马背上,成功地完成了原本做不到的事情,咧开小嘴露出了胜利的笑容。看到这一切,我也为她感到高兴。课上,我牵着"条纹"绕着马场走步,轻声地训练着马和马背上的骑士,教练在圆圈的中心引导着整支马队。我们时而慢走时而小跑,一起运动了一个小时。随着马儿有韵律的动作,凯蒂的身体也渐渐放松,与马儿动作一致,浑然一体。

在一片肃静中,辛酸的交流在凯蒂和"条纹"之间无声展开。出于本能,"条纹"异常敏感,他凭直觉感觉到凯蒂坐在马鞍里有点不平衡或是不舒服,于是它下意识地放柔了步伐。尽管凯蒂不能用马儿可以识别的语言来发出口令,但是"条纹"会通过判断凯蒂的语调来调整步伐。惊讶、高兴、犹豫、害怕,"条纹"都能领会而且能亲切地、耐心地做出反应,像是一个很棒的老师。

下课的时候,我帮助凯蒂下马,她的小脸蛋红扑扑的,笑得阳光灿烂,她用自己细细的胳膊围绕着"条纹"低下来的脖子。"条纹"一直低着头,凯蒂把脸埋在他的鬃毛里,柔柔地低语道:"我爱你,条纹。"我静静地站在几英尺之外,被这种不寻常的美所感动。

这种魔力吸引着我每周都来这里。每个星期六都不一样,治疗马和小骑士的轮换让志愿者们有机会了解每一匹马和每一个孩子。每个星期六我都会强烈地感受到一种马和人精神上的紧密联系。每个星期六都向我揭示了一种力量,那就是这神奇的4条腿的生物战胜了孩子们身体上或智力上的不幸。每个星期六,孩子们都能握住自由的缰绳和拥有一对珀加索斯的翅膀。

做志愿者这段个人旅程让我体会到了意想不到的丰富充实和鼓舞人心的感觉。帮助这些小孩子在另一种只有他们的马儿可以为他们创造的自然和精神王国里康复,看着这些孩子在他们的伙伴马儿的陪伴下获得力量,重新生活,我又一次发现了我对马的深爱,并且从他们温和的方式

that giving yields greater generosity than it asks.

Inspired by my experience,I picked up the phone one day and called my brother at the family farm where I had spent my teenage years."How's Cowboy doing?"I asked of my own horse.

"He's just fine,"my brother replied,"but I think he feels a bit forgotten."

And that's why,a week later,Cowboy came out of semiretirement and was transported to his new home hundreds of miles away—with me.Now Cowboy—my retired showhorse with huge brown eyes,a stripe down his back and a penchant for pleasing people—volunteers, too.

Vera Nicholas-Gervais

中体会到很多东西。最后,也是最重要的是,我认识到了付出会比索取收获更多的慷慨。

在这段经历的启发下,终于有一天我拿起电话打给了我的哥哥,他在我们家的农场工作,我也曾在家庭农场度过了我的少年时光。"牛仔怎么样啦?"我问起我自己的那匹马。

"他好着呢,"哥哥回答道,"不过我想他感到有人把他忘记了。"

这就是为什么牛仔在一个星期之后走出了他半退休状态的生活被转运到百里之外的他的新家,来到了我的身边。现在,我的牛仔,一只有着大大的棕色眼睛、背上有一道条纹的表演马,把欢乐带给了每一个人。

注释:珀加索斯:希腊神话中有双翼的飞马。

You Can't Afford to Doubt Yourself
你承担不起怀疑自我的后果

The fear of rejection is worse than rejection itself.

Nora Profit

对被拒绝的恐惧比被拒绝本身更糟糕。

诺拉·普罗菲特

On a spring evening some years ago,while living in New York,I decided to take in an off-Broadway musical where I heard Salome Bey sing for the first time.I was enthralled.I believed I had just discovered the next Sarah Vaughn.

The moment was magical.Even though half the seats were empty, Salome's voice filled the room and brought the theater to life.I had never witnessed anything quite like it.I was so moved by Salome's performance,yet disappointed about the sparse audience,I decided to write an article to help promote her.

Struggling to contain my excitement,the next day I phoned the theater where Salome Bey was appearing and unabashedly acted like

几年前一个春天的夜晚,那时我还住在纽约,我决定去观看一场非百老汇戏剧界的音乐喜剧。在那里,我第一次听到了萨洛米·贝的演唱。我被迷住了。我相信自己刚巧发现了萨拉·沃恩第二。

那是个神奇的时刻。尽管一半的座位都空着,萨洛米的声音还是充满了整个空间,给剧院注入了生机。我从未目睹像这样完美的表演。我被萨洛米的表演深深地打动了,出于对观众的稀少感到失望,我决定写篇稿子促使她走红。

第二天,我努力抑制住激动之情,给萨洛米演出的剧院打了个电话,

a professional writer:

"May I speak with Salome Bey,please?"

"Just one moment,please."

"Hello,this is Salome."

"Miss Bey,this is Nora Profit.I'm writing an article for *Essence* magazine,spotlighting your singing achievements.Is it possible for us to meet so that we might talk about your career?"

Did I say that?Essence is going to have me arrested, I thought.I don't know a thing about her singing achievements.My inner voice shouted,You have really done it this time!

"Why,of course,"said Salome. "I'm cutting my fourth album next Tuesday.Why don't you meet me at the studio?And bring along your photographer."

Bring my photographer! I thought,my confidence fading rapidly. I've really tied myself in a noose this time.I don't even know anyone who owns a camera.

"While I'm thinking about it,"continued Salome, "Galt McDermot, producer of *Hair,Dude and Highway Life* will be performing a benefit with me at the Staten Island Church-on-the-Hill. So why don't you plan to come to that,too,and I'll introduce you to him."

"Umm—of course,"I said,trying to sound professional. "That will add an extra dimension to the article."

An extra dimension?How would you know? snapped the nagging voice in my head.

"Thank you,Miss Bey,"I said,bringing the inquiry to a close. "I'll see you next Tuesday."

When I hung up,I was scared out of my mind.I felt as though I had jumped into a pool of quicksand and was about to be swallowed up with no chance at salvaging my dignity.

The next few days flashed by quickly.I made an emergency run

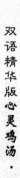

to the library.*Who is this Galt McDermot anyway?* And I frantically searched for anyone with a 35mm camera.A real photographer was out of the question.After all,I had spent all my extra cash on the Broadway theater ticket.

厚脸皮地佯装自己是一名专业作家。

"请问我能和萨洛米通话吗?"

"请稍等片刻。"

"你好,我是萨洛米。"

"贝小姐,我是诺拉·普罗菲特。我正在为《精华》杂志写一篇稿子,显示您的歌唱成就的亮点。我们能否见个面,谈谈您的事业生涯?"

我真那么说了吗?《精华》杂志社会让警察逮捕我的,我想道。我对她的歌唱成就一无所知。我内在的声音大声呼喊,你这次真的做到了!

"噢,当然罗,"萨洛米说,"我下周二录制我的第四张唱片。我们在录音室见面如何?别忘了带上你的摄影师。"

带上我的摄影师!我想着,自信一下子消失了。我这回真的为自己套上绞索了。我连一个有照相机的人都不认识。

"让我想一想,"萨洛米接着说,"高尔特·麦克德莫特,电影《头发》《花花公子与高速公路上的生活》的制片人,将会和我在斯塔腾岛的山上教堂举办一场慈善义演。你也去那里吧,我会把你介绍给他的。"

"嗯——当然,"我说,尽力让人听起来专业。"那会给这篇文章增加一个新的视角。"

新视角?你怎么知道?我脑子里那个恼人的声音呵斥道。

"谢谢你,贝小姐,"我说,准备将询问结束。"下周二再见。"

当我挂上电话时,我吓得魂不附体。我觉得像是跳进了一个满是流沙的池塘,即将被吞没却没有任何可以挽救命运的机会。

接下来的几天一闪而过。我紧急跑到图书馆。究竟高尔特·麦克德莫特是何许人?我急于寻找一个拥有35毫米照相机的人。毫无疑问,真正的摄影家是找不到的。毕竟,我把我所有的余款都用来买百老汇剧院的戏票了。

Then I lucked out.I learned my friend Barbara had become quite an accomplished photographer,so after I begged and pleaded,Barbara agreed to accompany me to the interview.

At both the recording session and the church benefit,Barbara clicked away,while I,a bundle of nerves,sat there looking very pensive,taking notes on a yellow pad,asking questions that all began with,"Can you tell me..."

Soon it was all over,and once outside the church,I ran frantically down the street,wanting to hail an ambulance because I thought I was going to die from the stress.I hailed a taxi instead.

Safe at home,I calmed down and began writing.But with every word I wrote,a small,stern voice inside me kept scolding:You lied! You're no writer! You haven't written anything.Why,you've never even written a good grocery list.You'll never pull this off!

I soon realized that fooling Salome Bey was one thing,but faking a story for *Essence*,a national magazine,was impossible. The pressure was almost unbearable.

Putting my heart into it,I struggled for days with draft after draft—rewriting and reediting my manuscript countless times. Finally, I stuffed my neatly typed,double-spaced manuscript into a large envelope,added my SASE (self-addressed stamped envelope),and dropped the package into a mailbox.As the mailman drove away,I wondered how long it would take before I'd get the *Essence* editor's unqualified "YUCK! "reply.

It didn't take long.Three weeks later there it was,my manuscript—returned in an envelope with my own handwriting. What an insult! I thought.How could I have ever thought that I could compete in a world of professional writers who make their living writing?How stupid of me!

Knowing I couldn't face the rejection letter with all the reasons why the editor hated my manuscript,I threw the unopened envelope into the nearest closet and promptly forgot about it,chalking up the

就在这时，我逢凶化吉。我得知我的朋友芭芭拉已经是个小有名气的摄影家了，于是在我诚恳的乞求下，芭芭拉同意陪我参加这次会面。

在录音和教会义演的过程中，芭芭拉不停地按动快门，而我则神经高度紧张地坐在那里，在一个黄色的便笺簿上做着记录，极度紧张不安，问的问题全部以"你能不能告诉我……"开头。

很快，所有这一切都结束了。一走出教堂，我就慌张地跑到街上，想招呼一辆救护车，因为我觉得自己快被这压力压得要死去了。然而我还是改变了主意，叫了一辆出租车。

在安全地回到家后，我镇定下来，开始写作。可我每写一个字，脑子里就有一个小声而严厉的声音在不停地斥责我：你撒谎！你根本不是作家！你从未写过任何作品。哎哟，你连一份令人满意的杂货店购物清单都不曾写过。你根本不可能做成这件事情！

我很快意识到欺骗萨洛米·贝仅仅是一个方面，而捏造一篇国家级刊物《精华》杂志上的故事却根本不可能。这种压力几乎达到令人难以承受的地步。

我全身心地投入写作，花若干天时间努力写了一遍又一遍——原稿经过了无数次的重写和修订。最后，我把打印得整整齐齐、双倍行间距的稿件塞进一个大信封里，附上我的SASE（寄给自己的贴好邮票的信封），然后把包裹投入邮箱。当邮递员开走邮车时，我就在想，到获得《精华》杂志社编辑寄来的斩钉截铁的回复"讨厌！"时，还要等待多长时间呢？

我并没等待多久。3周后我的稿件就被退回来了——放在那个由我自己写好地址的信封里。这是多大的羞辱！我想道。我当初怎么会幻想自己能够在一个由以写作为生的专业作家组成的世界里竞争呢？我多蠢哪！

我知道自己不敢面对这封退稿信，也不愿了解编辑讨厌这篇稿件的全部理由，于是，我把未启封的信扔进最近的橱柜里，然后迅速忘却了这件事。仅仅作为一次令人不愉快的经历，记下了这一整个痛苦的经验。

whole ordeal as a bad experience.

Five years later,while cleaning out my apartment preparing to move to Sacramento,California,to take a job in sales,I came across an unopened envelope addressed to me in my own handwriting.*Why would I send myself a package?*I thought.To clear up the mystery,I quickly opened the envelope and read the editor's letter in disbelief:

> *Dear Ms. Profit,*
> *Your story on Salome Bey is fantastic.We need some additional quotes.Please add those and return the article immediately.We would like to publish your story in the next issue.*

Shocked,it took me a long time to recover.Fear of rejection cost me dearly.I lost at least five hundred dollars and having my article appear in a major magazine—proof I could be a professional writer. More importantly,fear cost me years of enjoyable and productive writing.Today,I am celebrating my sixth year as a full-time freelance writer with more than one hundred articles sold.Looking back on this experience,I learned a very important lesson:

You can't afford to doubt yourself.

Nora Profit

5年后，当我清扫公寓准备搬往加利福尼亚州的萨克拉门托去接受一份营销工作时，我偶然发现了一封未启封的寄给我的信，信封上的地址是我自己的笔迹写的。为什么我会给自己寄包裹？我想道。为解开这个谜团，我快速地拆开信封，带着疑问阅读起编辑的回信：

亲爱的普罗菲特女士，

您写的关于萨洛米·贝的故事很奇妙。我们需要一些补充的引文。请加上那些引文然后立即将稿件寄回。我们将在下期刊出您写的故事。

令人震惊！许久我才从震惊中恢复过来。对被拒绝的恐惧让我付出了昂贵的代价。我失去了至少500美元的稿费，失去了让我的文章发表在一本重要杂志上的机会——那将证明我有能力成为一个专业作家。更重要的是，恐惧令我失去了愉快的年华和多产的写作。今天，当我庆祝自己成为全职自由作家6周年的时候，我已发表了上百篇文章。回顾这次经历，我得到了一个非常重要的教训：

你承担不起怀疑自我的后果。

A Guy Named Bill
有个男孩名叫比尔

His name was Bill.He had wild hair,wore a T-shirt with holes in it,blue jeans and no shoes.In the entire time I knew him I never once saw Bill wear a pair of shoes.Rain,sleet or snow,Bill was barefoot. This was literally his wardrobe for his whole four years of college.

He was brilliant and looked like he was always pondering the esoteric.He became a Christian while attending college.Across the street from the campus was a church full of well-dressed,middle-class people.They wanted to develop a ministry to the college students,but they were not sure how to go about it.

One day,Bill decided to worship there.He walked into the church, complete with his wild hair,T-shirt,blue jeans and bare feet.The church was completely packed,and the service had already begun.Bill started down the aisle to find a place to sit.By now the people were looking a bit uncomfortable,but no one said anything.

As Bill moved closer and closer to the pulpit,he realized there were no empty seats.So he squatted and sat down on the carpet right up front.(Although such behavior would have been perfectly acceptable at the college fellowship,this was a scenario this particular congregation had never witnessed before!) By now,the people seemed uptight, and the tension in the air was thickening.

Right about the time Bill took his "seat,"a deacon began slowly making his way down the aisle from the back of the sanctuary.The deacon was in his eighties,had silver gray hair,a three-piece suit and a pocket watch.He was a godly man—very elegant,dignified and courtly. He walked with a cane and,as he neared the boy,church members thought,"You can't blame him for what he's going to do.How can you expect a man of his age and background to understand some college kid on the floor?"

It took a long time for the man to reach the boy.The church was utterly silent except for the clicking of his cane.You couldn't even hear anyone breathing.All eyes were on the deacon.

他叫比尔。一头蓬松的头发,穿着一件满是破洞的T恤和一件蓝色牛仔裤,光着脚丫。自我认识他以来就从没见他穿过一双鞋。无论是雨天还是冰雪天,比尔总是赤着脚。这就是他4年大学生活的全部衣装。

他很聪明,看上去就好像是一个爱动脑子思考深奥问题的孩子。在上大学的时候他就成了基督徒。走出校园穿过大街是一所教堂,里面挤满了穿着体面的中产阶层的人们。他们想找一个合适的方式向大学生宣教,但是一时还不知道怎么做。

一天,比尔决定去教堂祷告。他依然是平时的打扮,蓬松的头发,破旧的T恤,蓝色牛仔裤,光着脚丫,不修边幅地走进教堂。里面已经坐满了人,礼拜仪式已经开始了。沿着教堂的过道,比尔想找一个地方坐下来。这时旁边的人看着他觉得有点不舒服,不过也没人说什么。

当比尔向讲道坛越挪越近时,他发现一个空位也没有了。于是他就蹲了下来席地而坐,这和在前面也不差多少。(尽管这种行为在大学里能被完全接受,但在教堂聚会这种特殊场合还是从未有过的!)这时候有些人看起来很生气,气氛越来越紧张。

就在比尔刚坐定,一位教堂执事缓慢地从后面的内殿往过道这边走来。执事80多岁了,一头银灰色的头发,一身3件套礼服,胸前佩着一只怀表。他是一个虔诚的基督徒,非常谦逊优雅,彬彬有礼。老人挂着一根手杖,就在他往比尔这边走过来的时候,其他人就在想:"也难怪执事要去找他,以他的年龄和身份怎么能够理解一个大学生坐在地上?"

过了很长时间,老人才走到男孩跟前。教堂里除了拐杖落地的声音外,其他一点声音也没有。人们屏气凝神,所有的目光都定格在执事的身上。

But then they saw the elderly man drop his cane on the floor. With great difficulty, he sat down on the floor next to Bill and worshipped with him. Everyone in the congregation choked up with emotion. When the minister gained control, he told the people, "What I am about to preach, you will never remember. What you've just seen, you will never forget."

可是人们看着老人却把手杖丢在了地上。他费力地在比尔旁边席地而坐和他一起祷告起来,这让全体参加圣会的人不觉心头颤动,哽咽不能语。当牧师安定下来以后,他告诉人们,"我下面将布道些什么,你们也许不会记住的。但今天你们所看到的这一幕,相信你们永远也忘不了。"

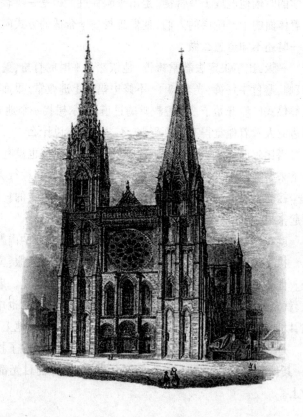

Father and Son
父与子

Writing,painting or music can often capture the splendor of the best of life,but occasionally life mirrors art.An experience occurred recently that brought this home to me:　Our student son Mark and I enjoyed a round of seaside golf near the Giant's Causeway in Northern Ireland—one of the most beautiful coastlines in the world.

I write not as a good golfer in the technical sense,but hopefully as a"good" player who enjoys a round in the company of family or friends,who tries hard to win but who doesn't mind losing to the better golfer.Sadly,"good golfers" in that sense are becoming harder to find in a competitive world.

Mark and I were intent on enjoying a day out together,one of those rare occasions where a father and son can share each other's company totally without interruption.Mark had just returned from a

写作、绘画和音乐可以经常捕捉到生活中最美好的那一瞬间,但在偶尔情况下生活却能反映艺术。最近的一次经历让我对此有了更深的感触。我和我正在读书的儿子迈克在北爱尔兰的巨人公路附近进行了一局海边高尔夫,那里的海岸线是世界上最美丽的之一。

从纯技巧的角度来说,我的创作并不是作为一个优秀的高尔夫球手,但我希望作为一个"好"的球手可以在家人或朋友的陪伴下享受每一局。他尽全力去赢,但并不介意输给一个更好的球手。悲哀的是,这样意义下的"好高尔夫球手"在这个充满竞争的社会是日益难寻了。

我和迈克打算好好享受两人一天在外的生活, 这是极少的父亲与儿子完全相伴而没有打扰的情况。迈克刚刚结束在德国的假期打工,他的工作是在一家作料厂铲咖喱粉。他准备返回英格兰的曼彻斯特大学,而我决

vacation job in Germany,where he had been shoveling curry powder in a spice factory.He was about to return to the University of Manchester in England,and I was due to go back to my busy desk at Queen's University in Belfast the next morning.So we settled for a sharing of seaside golf.

Those people who do not understand golf should still read on.I'm not sure that I understand golf myself,or why grown men and women spend so much time,money and energy—and suffer so much anguish—in trying to knock a small white ball into a tiny hole in the ground using a long awkward—looking stick,and trying to do so in as few strokes as possible.It is more than a game: It is a lesson in life.I have seen mature men pale at the prospect of knocking in a final three—foot putt to win a match.Even worse,I know men who have found it hard to lose gracefully to their close friends,or to their own sons. Sometimes such winners are really the losers.

Despite all such angst,there is a totally irrational surge of satisfaction—sometimes peaking into joy—when the golf swing works well and that little white ball zooms down the fairway as if Jack Nicklaus himself had hit it.It was one of those great days of unexpected golfing successes when Mark and I strode along the fairways, bounded on one side by the picturesque River Bush.I had played this course for more than twenty years,but on this particular morning I realized that Mark was coming of age and was beating his father for the first time,fair and square.

As we walked and talked,my mind lingered on the theme of life imitating art,and particularly the art of that great and much—loved English poet Sir John Bet jeman,who captured the magic of"Seaside Golf":

> *How straight it flew,how long it flew,*
> *It cleared the rutty track,*

And soaring,disappeared from view
Beyond the bunker's back—
A glorious,sailing,bounding drive
That made me glad I was alive.

As our game progressed through the regulation eighteen holes,it

定第二天一早便要回到贝尔法斯特皇后大学繁忙的办公桌旁。所以我们决定一起去玩海边高尔夫球。

那些不懂高尔夫的人还是可以继续往下读。我自己都不确定自己是否懂得高尔夫,为什么成年的男性和女性花那么多时间,金钱和精力(还承受那么多痛苦),用一个长而难看的棍子努力地把一个小小的白球打进地上的一个小洞里,而且还要用尽可能少的击打次数。这已经不仅仅是一个游戏了:这是人生的一堂课。我曾经见过一个稳重的先生在最后将球击入3英尺外的洞内时脸色变得煞白。更有甚者,有些男人在输给自己亲密的朋友或儿子时,都会风度尽失。这样的人即使胜了,也更像个输家。

虽然有这么多苦恼,但是当你挥杆就像杰克·尼克拉斯一样让那个白色的小球在击球区上方呈弧线飞行,你就会体验到一种无法言表的满足感,到达欢乐的顶峰。当我和迈克在与风景如画的布什河相毗邻的击球区时,他出人意料地赢了我很多局,这是我最美好的回忆之一。我接触这项运动已经超过20年了,但是正在这个早上,我意识到迈克长大了,他第一次公平的赢了他的父亲。

当我们边走边聊的时候,我的思绪漂浮到生活模仿艺术的话题上,尤其是那位伟大的备受爱戴的英国诗人约翰·贝杰曼爵士,他捕捉到了"海边高尔夫"的魔力:

它飞得多直,飞得多远

它掠过遍地车辙,

昂扬,消失在视线

越过蹦跳着的小马的背脊

一次光荣的,航海般的,跳跃的历程

让我体会到生命的欢腾

was obvious that Dad,playing quite well by his standards,was hanging on for dear life.And at the very last hole,Mark,a gentle giant of a young man,strode forward none-too-confidently to try to sink a short putt that would win the match.As he stood there concentrating,I wanted him to sink the putt and win,but I was equally prepared to play on to a"sudden death" if necessary.Agonizingly he hit it,and the ball rolled gently—into the cup! A beam of joy lit up his face,and I felt deep in my heart:"That's my boy."I thought,too,of the lines of Betjeman:

> *It lay content*
> *Two paces from the pin:*
> *A steady putt and then it went*
> *Oh,most securely in.*
> *The very turf rejoiced to see*
> *That quite unprecedented three.*

Afterwards,in the clubhouse,we had a simple but splendid lunch overlooking the very green where Mark had clinched his memorable victory.We replayed every stroke,we talked about sport and we philosophized about life.I even pointed out,for the umpteenth time,the sparkling white hotel across the headlands where his mother and I had held our wedding reception a quarter century earlier,and I told him,yet again,of my early and troubled attempts to learn to play golf on this very same course.One day I became so frustrated that I put the ball in my pocket and walked on with my partner,rather than try to play a few holes.Later,my editor,when reading of this in my Belfast newspaper column,wrote the following headline: "The Day I Played Four Holes in None! "

Mark,for his part,listened intently and appreciatively to this family history.He too has an eye for beauty and an ear for poetry.He is (I'll say it) a treasured son,a partner and confidant in his own right, and his triumph on the golf course had underlined his maturity and growing sense of independence.With such a son I,technically the loser,

当我们的游戏进入到例行的18个洞的阶段，正常水平发挥下的爸爸已经很明显的几乎胜券在握了。在最后一个洞口的时候，文雅高大的年轻人迈克仍然不卑不亢地向前迈一步,想要用短短的一击将球击入而获胜。当他集中注意力站在那里的时候,我真希望他能击中赢得比赛,但是我也准备如果必要的话给自己来一场"突然死亡"。他沉着击球,球缓缓地滚动落入洞中!一丝喜悦闪过他的脸庞,我深深的感觉到:"这是我的孩子。"我又一次想起了贝杰曼的诗句:

> 它奠定内容
>
> 另两位来它奠定内容
>
> 两名来自桥牌密码
>
> 然后进入稳步推杆
>
> 哦,最稳妥的
>
> 很高兴见到草坪
>
> 这三个相当空前

之后我们在俱乐部会所共进了一顿简单却丰盛的午餐。从那儿我们可以俯瞰到那片草地。在那儿,迈克的获胜让人难忘。我们回顾了每一次击球,我们谈论运动,我们探讨生活的哲学。我甚至在无数次告诉他之后,又一次指给他看,那个穿过海峡的闪光的白色旅馆是25年前我和他妈妈举行婚礼盛宴的地方。我再一次告诉他正是这同一块场地见证了我早期进行高尔夫球运动艰辛的努力。有一天我实在是太累了,我没有打球,而是把球放在口袋里和搭档一起走进场地。之后,我的编辑读到了我在贝尔法斯特报纸上的专栏,写下了这样的标题:"我击4杆而一球未进的一天!"

迈克认真而欣赏地听着他爸爸的这段经历。他对于美与诗也有自己的鉴赏力。他是(我即将要说)我宝贝的儿子,有独立主见的搭档和密友,而且他在高尔夫球场上的胜利更是加深了他的成熟和逐渐独立的意识。拥有这样一个儿子,我,作为技巧上的失败者,欣慰地明白,从更深的角度

knew that I was,happily,a long-term winner in a much deeper way.

That night,I read to Mark the last stanza of the Betjeman poem that recaptured so beautifully our feelings of privilege and joy.

> *Ah! seaweed smells from sandy caves*
> *And thyme and mist in whiffs,*
> *In coming tide,Atlantic waves*
> *Slapping the sunny cliffs,*
> *Lark song and sea sounds in the air,*
> *And splendor,splendor everywhere.*

Indeed.There had been enough splendor on that fine day to warm the hearts of a father and a son for a lifetime.

Alf McCreary

上来说,我是一个长远的胜者。

那天晚上,我给迈克读贝杰曼《滨海高尔夫》的最后一节,这首诗再次捕捉到我们的殊荣与喜悦的美妙情感。

> 啊!沙石洞穴中飘出海草的味道
> 和着百里香的薄雾,
> 自远处袭来的潮汐,大西洋的波浪
> 惊涛拍岸,溅在阳光下的绝壁,
> 云雀在歌唱,大海在欢笑,
> 空中,地上到处弥漫着壮观和杰出。

的确,那美妙一天的辉煌足以终生温暖一个父亲和儿子的心。

Anna Mae's Honor
安娜·迈尔的信誉

Can it really be thirty years since I received the last of the payments from Annie Mae? I find myself thinking about them more often as I approach my sixtieth birthday. Something about closing the chapters on six decades and opening the pages of a new one makes one reflect.

Annie Mae's life has deeply touched mine. I first met her at the home of my in-laws in 1959. I had moved with my husband and our one-year-old child to Tuscaloosa, Alabama, so my husband could complete his undergraduate work at the University of Alabama. My father-in-law was a professor of finance at the university, and my mother-in-law was active in university and community affairs. I vividly recall entering their driveway and being overwhelmed by the size of their home, the beauty of the furnishings, the manicured grounds and the pecan orchard.

自从收到安娜·迈尔的最后一笔欠款,到现在,真的已经有30年了吗?

在我60岁生日即将到来之际,我发现自己会更经常地想到他们。我人生前60年的生活结束了,又一段新生活即将开始,此时此刻,我不禁要深思一些事情。

安娜的生活曾经深深地感动了我。1959年,我在夫家初次遇到了安娜。那时为了便于我丈夫能够完成在阿拉巴马州的本科学业,我和丈夫连同我们一岁的儿子搬到了亚拉巴马的托卡路撒。我的公公是该大学的一位财经学教授,婆婆也积极参与该大学和社区的社会事务。我至今仍能清楚地记得当初驶入他们家的路车道,看到他们巨大房子时的震惊,更能记得他们家美丽的家装,修剪整齐的草坪和风景优美的核桃园。

Annie Mae was my in-law's maid.She prepared and served meals in her quiet,gentle way and then returned to the kitchen to read her Bible while we ate.She was a dedicated and devoted Christian.To me, she reflected the fruit of the Holy Spirit as found in Galatians 5:22-23. I found this increasingly true even though I came to know her more by observation than by conversation.

My husband and I visited his parents frequently,and I became increasingly taken with this gentle,remarkable lady.Often when I saw her eating alone,reading her Bible,I wanted to sit down with her and just talk.However,whites did not do that with African Americans in the South in those days,and I conformed to the local practice— though it conflicted with my Christian beliefs.I watched my son,Jimmy, play with her daughter,Jennifer Ann,who on occasion came to my in-laws' place with her mother.

The two children laughed and frolicked amid the trees in the pecan orchard.It was so easy for them.

In 1965,my world was suddenly uprooted.I found myself alone with two young sons when my husband wanted a divorce.I was fortunate to receive a full scholarship to the University of Connecticut in the field of special education.I decided to sell the furniture and household items and return to my home state with just our clothes.

Annie Mae asked if she could buy the boys' beds.When I answered yes,she asked the price. "Thirty-five dollars,"I replied.Then,in her quiet way,she asked if I would sell them to her and trust her to send a little money each month.I admired her and knew her to be a woman of God,trustworthy and honest.The words of Proverbs 11 came to mind:"A good man [person] is guided... and directed by honesty... Be sure you know a person well before you vouch for his [or her] credit."

Annie Mae was honest,and I knew her well.So I said,"Annie Mae, take them,they are yours."

I returned to Connecticut with my two sons and found a chicken coop that had been converted into four apartments.My neighbors and

安娜·迈尔是我夫家的女佣,每天她平静而温柔地为全家准备着一日三餐,然后,在我们就餐时,她会回到厨房读她的《圣经》。她是个虔诚的基督徒,我认为她完全具备了《加拉太书》里面第5章第22~23节所提到的那些美德。(这些美德指的是仁爱、喜乐、和平、忍耐、恩慈、善良、信实、温柔、节制。)

我和丈夫经常去看望他的父母,我也越加被这位温柔而不同寻常的女士所吸引。每每我见她独自一人边吃边看《圣经》时,我就想坐下来和她聊聊。但在当时白人不能与黑人这么交往,我只能遵守当地的法律——尽管这与我的基督徒信仰相冲突。有时她也带着女儿杰妮弗来我夫家,我儿子吉米和杰妮弗在一起玩的时候我总在一旁驻足观望。

两个孩子在核桃园中尽情地嬉戏玩耍,他们才不去理会那些清规戒律。

1965年,我的生活突然发生了变化。丈夫提出与我离婚,我只能与自己的两个幼子相依为伴。幸运的是,我收到了一份来自康涅狄格州大学的特殊教育领域的全额奖学金。我决意卖掉家具和其他家用品,只带着我们的衣物回了老家。

安娜问我,她是否能买下我儿子们睡的床。我说可以,她就又问多少钱能卖。我说35元。她仍平静地问,她是否能以每月支付一点钱的方式来付款。实际上,我很钦佩她,我知道她是上帝的真正子民——诚实,值得信任。《箴言》11章上的话出现在我的脑海中,"正直人的纯正,必引导自己……在你为别人担保前,要弄清这人是否值得信任。"

我十分了解安娜,她很诚实。因此我说,"安娜,拿去吧,它们属于你的了。"

我带着我的两个儿子回到了康涅狄格州,这儿原先是一个鸡舍的地方现在已成了4个公寓住所。我和邻居在努力获得学位的同时关系也亲近起来了。我和孩子们住在这儿时,每个月都能收到安娜的一封信,里面装

I all became family as we struggled to earn our degrees.Faithfully each month,while my boys and I lived there,an envelope arrived from Annie Mae—two dollars,three dollars,five dollars,always in cash.That became the surprise money for my boys; I used it to get them something special—an ice cream,cookies,an outing.My sons were thrilled when Annie Mae's money came,for they knew that a surprise would be coming their way.

A year passed.I earned my master of arts degree in special education and accepted a position as a special education teacher for the state of Connecticut.I had learned my lessons well.However,I was about to learn an even greater lesson,and Annie Mae would be the teacher.

Annie Mae's last payment arrived about the time I completed my studies.Along with it came the following note:

Dear Mrs.Holladay,
I am sending you my last payment of three dollars to pay for the beds in full.I told my two sons that they could now go to the storage shed and put the beds together and sleep in them, for they are now paid for and rightfully ours.Thank you for your trust.
Love in Jesus,
Annie Mae

I could not believe my eyes.I read the note two or three times, my eyes filling with tears.Had I only known earlier,I would have said, "Use them now.Don't wait until you pay for them."

Those would have been my thoughts,yet Annie Mae had other thoughts—thoughts the world could truly use.She sacrificed.She struggled.And finally,when the beds were truly hers,she let her sons,

Paul and John,sleep in them.She was a living example of absolute honesty,the honesty that should characterize all who claim to be Christian.

This story has a postscript.After thirty years,I called directory assistance and found that Annie Mae still lived in Tuscaloosa.I called

着2美元、3美元、5美元的现金。孩子们见到这些钱时十分惊喜,因为我用这些钱给他们买一些特别的东西,像一块冰淇淋,甜点心或是一次远足。每当安娜的钱寄来时,孩子们都异常高兴,因为他们知道又一个惊喜即将到来。

一年过去了,我获得了特殊教育的文学硕士学位,又在康涅狄格州谋得一个作为特殊教师的职位。我的功课学得不错,但当时我还不知道,我即将要修另一门更重要的课程,而安娜将是我的老师。

当我即将结束学业时,我收到安娜的最后一笔欠款。随附短信一封:

亲爱的赫拉戴夫人,

这是我购床所欠的最后3美元。现在我跟我的两个儿子说,他们可以从储藏室里把床取出来,拼装起来在上面睡觉了,因为我们已经付清了钱,这床理应属于我们的了。感谢你的信任。

内主平安

安娜

我简直不敢相信,把信又读了两三遍,眼里充满了泪水。如果我早知道的话,我会说,"用吧,不用等到付清钱再睡。"

这只是我的想法,然而安娜可能与我的想法不同,而我们这个世界正缺少她的这样的想法。她奉献,拼搏,最终当这张床真正属于她时,才同意孩子波尔和约翰睡。她是一个绝对诚实的活生生的例子,这样的诚实品质应该是所有自称是基督徒的人的共同特征。

这个故事并没就此结束。30年后,我打电话询问了电话查询处,得知安娜仍住在托卡路撒。我和她通了电话,然后我和我的第二任丈夫去看望

her,and later my second husband and I visited her,and I had that chat I never had thirty years ago.What a joy it was! Annie Mae had become a family and children's worker for the state of Alabama and retired in May of 1996.

Romans 13:8 says,"Pay all your debts except the debt of love for others,never finish paying that!"How Annie Mae reflects those words! Truly she is a remarkable woman,one whose life has been shaped by Bible principles.

了她,也就有了一场30年前没能有的交谈。真是太高兴了！安娜后来成了阿拉巴马州的"家庭与孩子"组织的社工,并于1996年5月也退休了。

《罗马书》13章第8节写道,"凡事都不可亏欠人,唯有彼此相爱,要常以为亏欠,因为爱人的,就完全了律法。"安娜就是践行了这些话。她的确是一个不简单的女人,她的一生都是按照《圣经》的要求来做的。

Bringing Your Heart to Work
用心工作

You can handle people more successfully by enlisting their feelings than by convincing their reason.

Paul P.Parker

打动情感比诉诸理智更能收服人心。

保罗·帕克

A corporate client subcontracted with me to train the major telemarketing firm she worked for.While training the telemarketing staff in sales,I noticed agitation among them.They were learning a new sales technology that combines trust,integrity and collaboration in supporting a prospect's buying decisions.They worked hard and were excited about learning,but it was obvious they were holding back their full commitment.By the end of the first day,I knew I couldn't continue without a full understanding of what was going on with the team.

"Is there a problem with you learning this technology?"I asked. They sat silently.I waited for an answer.Finally,someone spoke.

一位客户和我签订了转包合同，要我为她所服务的大型电话推销公司训练员工。我在向那些员工传授销售技巧时，却发现他们个个都焦虑不安。当时我传授的是一种结合信赖、诚信与合作，以增强消费者购买意念的技巧，学员们都很努力，学习动机也很强，但是很显然，他们不认为这种方法可以完全付诸实践。第一天课程结束时，我知道我必须弄清楚他们心中的想法，才能让课程继续下去。

"你们在学习这种技巧时，有什么问题吗?"我问，但他们一言不发地静坐着。我等着有人告诉我答案，终于，有人开口了。

"It would be great if we could really use this stuff.I mean,I can see where it would really work,and I wouldn't have to feel like I'm being so abusive to the people I'm calling.But I don't really think the company will let us use it.They don't care about people.They treat us like subhumans,use abusive selling tactics for prospects and only care about the bottom line.If they found out we were using this type of approach they'd put a stop to it."

I told the group I'd think about the problem and made a commitment to assist them in finding a way to integrate the new skills.They seemed to be happy to try,but unconvinced that I could make a difference.

Following the program,I went to the telephone bank where the salespeople worked and watched while the company's senior vice-president came over to speak with one of the representatives.He interrupted her in the middle of a conversation.He then walked over to another person who was on a sales call and asked him why he had a personal photo on his desk,since none were allowed.At the desk where I was sitting was a memo from the same man,telling people they had to wear suits the following day and keep their suit jackets on between 11:00 A.M.and noon because prospective clients would be coming through the office.

I waited until the senior vice-president went back to his office and knocked on his door.Since I teach collaboration,I decided to assume we were in a win-win situation.He smiled and invited me to speak. "I've got a problem that I'm hoping you can solve.I've been hired to teach this new sales technology that really supports trust and collaboration.However,the participants are afraid to bring it back to their desks."

He was a big man and an ex-Marine.He sat way back in his chair and rocked,smiling at me over a well-fed stomach.He replied, "If it makes money,why should they be afraid？"

I took a good look at the man.He seemed gentle,although his actions didn't indicate that."Do you mind if I ask you a really personal

"你所说的这些东西如果能实际运用当然很好,我的意思是说,我明白这些技巧可以运用在什么地方,让我在打电话给顾客的时候,不会感到那么不好意思。但是我想,公司一定不会让我们运用这引进的技巧。他们才不关心别人怎么想,也不把我们当人看,他们只会运用一些强迫性的推销技巧,只管每个人是不是达到基本业绩。如果他们发现我们在用这些技巧,一定会阻止的。"

我告诉来上课的学员,我会好好思考这个问题。我还答应他们,一定会想办法帮助他们实际运用这些新技巧。他们表面上看来乐于一试,不过实际上显然不太相信我会有什么办法。

课程结束后,我特别拜访这些学员工作的电话推销公司,并先在一旁观看。那家公司的一个资深副总裁走过来和其中一个学员代表说话,不过那个学员的话才说到一半,他就打断她,径自走到另一个正在打电话推销产品的学员身旁,问他为什么违反公司的规定,在桌上放置私人照片。我在所坐的位子四处观望,刚好有张那位副总裁发布的命令,要全公司的员工第二天早上11点到12点,都得穿西装、打领带,因为有重要客户要到办公室来参观。

我等那位资深副总裁回到自己的办公室,才去敲他的门。由于我传授的是协调合作的技巧,我在心底暗自期许,希望这次谈话能够达到双赢的目的。他微笑着等我开口。我说:"我有个问题想请你帮我解决。我应邀来传授一种强调诚信与合作的销售新技巧,但是我班上的学员好像都不敢把这种技巧运用在实际工作上。"

这位资深副总裁从前当过海军陆战队员,身材相当高大。他向后靠进椅子里,挺胸凸肚子,一面摇晃椅子,一面微笑着看我,然后回答:"如果这种方法能赚钱,他们为什么不敢用呢！"

我仔细审视眼前这个人。他外表看来相当温文和善,但实际行动却不然。我问他:"我能不能问你一个私人问题?"他微笑的嘴更大了,一面摇着

question that may have nothing to do with anything?"I asked.His smile broadened and he nodded as he rocked.I felt his acceptance of me.

"How do you function at work each day when you leave your heart at home? "

The man continued to rock gently,never changing his expression. I watched while his eyes narrowed.He responded,"What else do you know about me? "

"It's confusing for me,"I ventured,"You seem to be a gentle person,yet your actions don't seem to take people into account.You're putting task before relationship,but somehow I think you know the difference."

He looked at his watch and asked,"Are you free for dinner? Come on,it's on me."

Our dinner lasted three hours.He graphically recounted his Vietnam experiences as an officer who had to do bad things to good people.He cried,I cried.His shame had kept him silent,and he had never discussed the experiences with anyone before.He spent his life believing that his goodness could hurt people,so he decided years before not to let his heart get in the way of his job.It was a pain he carried daily.His sharing gave me the permission to talk about one of my own pains in my life that I rarely shared.Together we sat with cold food,warm beers and tears.

The next morning he called me into his office. "Could you sit with me while I do something? " he asked.Then he called in the woman who had hired me,and apologized for not supporting her and for being disrespectful to her in front of others.She was shocked and grateful.He then turned to me and asked,"Is there anything else you think I should do? "

I thought for a moment and replied,"You may want to consider

双语精华版心灵鸡汤·

apologizing to the entire team."

Without hesitation,he picked up the phone and asked his secretary to call in the team for a quick meeting.There,he apologized to the client in front of the team,apologized to the team for being dis-

椅子,一面点头,我觉得他已经接受我了。

"你每天都把心留在家里,那你到办公室是怎么办公的?"

他眯起双眼,继续轻轻摇椅子,脸上的表情一点也没变,回答道:"你对我这个人,还知道些什么?"

"我觉得很奇怪,"我以试探性的语气说,"你看来是个很和善的人,但你的行为好像很少考虑到别人。对你来说,工作重于人际关系,但不知道为什么,我老觉得你应该明白这之间的差别。"

他看看表,然后问我:"你今天晚上有空吗?我们一起去吃饭吧! 我请客! "

那顿饭,我们吃了3小时。他提纲挈领地告诉我他在越南的经历。当时他担任军官,必须对很好的人做出很残忍的事情。说完后,他哭了,我也哭了。由于心中羞愧,他一直对于过去的那些事保持沉默,不敢对任何人谈起,但他这一生因此认定,自己的和善可能会对别人造成伤害,于是多年前他就暗下决心,绝不让自己的"心"妨碍自己的工作,他每天都承担着这种痛苦;而他的坦诚,也让我勇敢敞开胸怀,向他透露一件我很少向人提及的心中憾事。我们一起坐在那里,盘中食物渐凉,泪水与啤酒却温暖洋溢。

第二天早上,他把我叫进他的办公室。他问我:"我等一下要处理一些事情,你能不能坐在这里陪我一下?"然后他叫一开始和我签转包合同的那位女士进来,向她道歉,说过去没有给她充分支持,而且在别人面前对她不够尊重。那位女士又惊讶又感激。然后他转过来问我:"还有什么事情你认为我应该做?"

我想了想,然后回答:"你也许应该考虑向全体员工道歉。"

他毫不犹豫地拿起电话,请秘书召集全体员工,开个小小的会。他在会上当着员工的面,向那位职员道了歉,又向全体员工表示了歉意,说自

respectful to them,and offered to make whatever changes they needed,so that they would want to come in to work each day.He also wanted to learn my technology and offer it to his entire sales staff.

That was the first of several meetings between the senior vice-president,my client and the team.People who were looking for new jobs stopped looking.People began to trust that being at work wouldn't be harmful and might even be fun.The team supported the new collaborative sales approach.The senior vice-president began to use his new skills with other teams.And I got a new friend.

Sharon Drew Morgen

己先前对他们不够尊重,同时表示自己愿意做任何改变,好让员工每天都能高高兴兴地来上班。他还说他也想学习我的销售技巧,好把这种技巧传授给公司其他员工。

那次会议只是这位资深副总裁、我的客户以及整个工作小组召开的第一次会议,后来他们又开了好几次类似的会。原本在找其他工作的人,现在都不找了,这些人开始相信,努力不一定有害,而且还可能很有趣。整个小组都相当支持新的销售技巧,资深副总裁也开始把这种新技巧介绍给其他工作小组,而我则交到了一个新朋友。

The Perfect Mistake
美丽的失误

Grandpa Nybakken loved life—especially when he could play a trick on somebody.At those times,his large Norwegian frame shook with laughter while he feigned innocent surprise,exclaiming, "Oh, forevermore! "But on a cold Saturday in downtown Chicago,Grandpa felt that God played a trick on him,and Grandpa wasn't laughing.

Mother's father worked as a carpenter.On this particular day,he was building some crates for the clothes his church was sending to an orphanage abroad.On his way home,he reached into his shirt pocket to find his glasses,but they were gone.He remembered putting them there that morning,so he drove back to the church.His search proved fruitless.

When he mentally replayed his earlier actions,he realized what happened.The glasses had slipped out of his pocket unnoticed and

生命的彩虹

我的外公,纳巴肯,是一个热爱生活的老人。特别是在他跟别人开玩笑的时候,这一点体现得更为明显。每每这个时候,他那挪威人的高大身躯一边笑得前仰后合,一边假装毫不知情喊道:"天啦,再也别这样开玩笑了!"但是在芝加哥市中心一个阴冷的周六,外公感到上帝跟他开了一个大玩笑,这次他没有心情笑了。

外公是一个木匠。那天,他正为教堂做一些装货箱,用这些货箱来包装一些衣服运到国外的孤儿院。回家的路上,他把手伸到衬衫口袋里摸眼镜,结果发现眼镜不见了。他记得早晨就把它放在口袋里,于是他又折回到教堂,可是无果而返。

当他用心回忆早些时候做了些什么时,他才意识到是怎么回事。原来在他封箱的时候,眼镜不经意间滑落到一个装货箱里了。现在他的新眼镜

fallen into one of the crates,which he had nailed shut.His brand new glasses were heading for China!

The Great Depression was at its height,and Grandpa had six children.He had spent twenty dollars for those glasses that very morning.

"It's not fair,"he told God as he drove home in frustration. "I've been very faithful in giving of my time and money to your work,and now this."

Several months later,the director of the orphanage was on furlough in the United States.He wanted to visit all the churches that supported him,so he came to speak on Sunday night at my grandfather's small church in Chicago.Grandpa and his family sat in their customary seats among the sparse congregation.

"But most of all,"he said, "I must thank you for the glasses you sent last year."

"Even if I had the money,there was simply no way of replacing those glasses.Along with not being able to see well,I experienced headaches every day,so my coworkers and I were much in prayer about this.Then your crates arrived.When my staffed removed the covers,they found a pair of glasses lying on top."

The missionary paused long enough to let his words sink in. Then,still gripped with the wonder of it all,he continued: "Folks,when I tried on the glasses,it was as thought they had been custom-made just for me! I want to thank you for being a part of that! "

The people listened,happy for the miraculous glasses.But the missionary surely must have confused their church with another, they thought.There were no glasses on their list of items to be sent overseas.

But sitting quietly in the back,with tears streaming down his face,an ordinary carpenter realized the Master Carpenter had used

双
语
精
华
版
心
灵
鸡
汤
·

him in an extraordinary way.

正在运往中国的路上。

当时正值大萧条最不景气的时候,外公又有6个孩子。他那天早晨刚花20美元买了那副眼镜。

"这真是太不公平了,"驾车回去的路上他沮丧地埋怨道。"主啊!对于你赐予我的工作,我已经够虔诚地奉献了我的时间和金钱,可现在却落得这样。"

几个月以后,孤儿院院长来美国休假。他想参观所有给过他帮助的美国教堂,于是在星期天晚上他来到芝加哥我外公他们的小教堂。外公和他的一家人坐在稀疏的会众中,他们一贯坐的位子上。

"重要的是,我必须感谢你们去年邮寄给我们的那副眼镜。"

"即使我有钱,也实在没办法买到那样的眼镜。就这样除了看不清,每天还要忍受头疼的煎熬,所以我和我的同事每天都在祈祷能有一副眼镜。后来你们的装货箱抵达了。当工人打开盖子的时候,一副眼镜就平放在衣服的上面。"

传教士停顿了一会儿,好让别人完全理解他的意思。他接着说道,仍然感触于这个不可思议的奇迹:"各位,当我戴上它以后,它简直就像是为我定做的! 我太感谢你们了!"

人们仔细聆听着,为这副眼镜神奇般出现而高兴。但是他们想传教士一定是把这个教堂与另外一家教堂搞混淆了。因为在他们捐向海外的物品清单中根本没有眼镜。

但是静静坐在后面的一个普通木匠却心情复杂,他的眼泪情不自禁地流了下来。他终于明白,主利用一个不同寻常的方式使用了他。(译者注:这里说到Master Carpenter,因为耶稣曾是木匠。)

The Last Straw
最后一根稻草

Let us think about each other and help each other to show love and do good deeds.

Heb.10:24

让我们互相牵挂,互相帮助,向别人表现出我们的爱,为别人做好事。

希伯莱书第10章24节

It was another long,winter afternoon with everyone stuck in the house.And the four McDonald children were at it again—bickering, teasing,fighting over their toys.At times like these,Mother was almost ready to believe that her children didn't love each other,though she knew that wasn't really true.All brothers and sisters fight,of course, but lately her lively little bunch had been particularly horrible to each other,especially Eric and Kelly,who were just a year apart.They seemed determined to spend the whole winter making each other miserable.

"Gimme that.It's mine! "

"Is not,fatso! I had it first! "

Mother sighed as she listened to the latest argument coming from the living room.With Christmas only a month away,the McDonald house seemed sadly lacking in Christmas spirit.This was supposed to be the season of sharing and love,of warm feelings and happy hearts. A home needed more than just pretty packages or twinkling lights on the tree to fill it with the Christmas spirit.But how could any mother convince her children that being kind to each other was the most important way to get ready for Christmas?

Mother had only one idea.Years ago her grandmother had told her about an old Christmas custom that helped people discover the real meaning of Christmas.Perhaps it would work for her family.It was worth a try.Mother gathered her four little rascals together and sat them down on the stairs,smallest to tallest—Mike,Randi,Kelly and Eric.

"How would you kids like to start a new Christmas project this year?"she asked."It's like a game,but it can only be played by people

这是又一个漫长的冬季下午,每一个人都挤在屋子里,麦克唐纳家的4个孩子也不例外,他们又像往常一样——互相斗嘴,嘲弄,为玩具争吵。每当这个时候,母亲几乎要相信她的孩子根本没有爱着彼此,虽然她知道并不是这样。当然天下所有的兄弟姐妹都会吵架,但是她可爱的小孩子们似乎对待彼此尤其糟糕,特别是艾瑞克和凯丽,他们岁数相差一年。他们似乎决意要在整个冬天都不给对方好日子过。

"把那个给我。它是我的!"

"它才不是你的,胖子!我先得到它的!"

母亲听到从客厅传来的最近的这次争吵时叹了口气。圣诞节还有一个月就要来临了,麦克唐纳家看上去根本没有圣诞气氛。圣诞被认为是一个让爱、温暖的情感和喜悦的心共同分享的季节。家里需要的不仅仅是精美包装的礼物和点缀在圣诞树上闪烁的灯光来增加节日的氛围。可是母亲到底怎样才能说服她的孩子们,友善地对待彼此是为圣诞做准备的最重要的方式呢?

母亲只有一个主意。多年以前,她的祖母告诉过她可以帮助人们发现圣诞的真正意义的古老传统。大概这也能够帮助她的家庭。这值得一试。母亲召集来她的四个小淘气鬼,让他们坐在台阶上,从矮到高——迈克,让迪,凯丽和艾瑞克。

"孩子们,你们觉得我们今年来一个新的圣诞项目怎么样呢?"她问

who can keep a secret.Can everyone here do that?"

"I can! "shouted Eric,wildly waving his arm in the air.

"I can keep a secret better than he can,"yelled Kelly,jumping up and waving her arm in the air,too.If this was a contest,Kelly wanted to make sure she beat Eric.

"I can do it! "chimed in Randi,not quite sure what was happening but not wanting to be left out.

"Me too,me too,me too."squealed little Mike,bouncing up and down.

"Well then,here's how the game works,"Mother explained. "This year we're going to surprise Baby Jesus when he comes on Christmas Eve by making him the softest bed in the world.We're going to build a little crib for him to sleep in right here in our house,and we'll fill it with straw to make it comfortable.But here's the catch:Each piece of straw we put in the manger will represent one kind thing we do for someone between now and Christmas.The more kind things we do, the more straw there will be for the Baby Jesus.The secret part is— we can't tell anyone what good things we're doing and who we're do- ing them for."

The children looked confused."How will Baby Jesus know it's his bed?"asked Kelly.

"He'll know,"said Mother. "He'll recognize it by the love we've put into the crib,by how soft it is."

"But who will we do the kind things for?"asked Eric.

"It's simple,"said Mother. "We'll do them for each other.Once every week between now and Christmas,we'll put all of our names in this hat,mine and Daddy's,too.Then we'll each draw a name and do kind things for that person for a whole week.But here's the hard part. We can't tell anyone whose name we've drawn for that week,and we'll each try to do as many favors as we can for our special person without getting caught.And for every secret good thing we do,we'll put another piece of straw in the crib."

"But what if I pick someone I don't like?"frowned Kelly.

Mother thought about that for a minute. "Maybe you could use

道,"这像个游戏,但只有会保守秘密的人才能玩。你们有人能做好吗？"

"我可以！"艾瑞克叫起来,拼命地挥舞着他的胳膊。

"我会比他更好地保守秘密,"凯丽叫道,她蹦着跳着,也在空中挥舞着手臂。如果这是个比赛,她希望能确保自己击败艾瑞克。

"我能做到！"让迪吵起来,虽然还不太清楚是怎么回事,但显然也不想落后。

"我也是,我也是,我也是,"迈克尖叫着,上蹦下跳。

"好,下面是这个游戏的规则,"母亲解释说。"今年我们打算在圣诞节前夕耶稣宝宝来的时候给他一个惊喜,我们要给他做一张世界上最软的床。我们打算在房子的这里给他建一个小婴儿床让他睡觉,我们要在床上铺满稻草使他更加舒适。但关键在这儿:我们放进马槽里的每一根稻草都要代表我们从现在到圣诞节为某一个人做的好事。好事做得越多,耶稣宝宝得到的稻草就越多。需要保密的部分是——我们不能告诉任何人我们做了什么好事以及为谁做的。"

孩子们看上去很迷惑。"耶稣宝宝怎么知道这是他的床呢？"凯丽问道。

"他会知道的,"母亲说,"他会从婴儿床里的爱和柔软认出它。"

"但是我们该为谁做好事呢？"艾瑞克问。

"这很简单,"妈妈说。"我们为彼此做。从现在起到圣诞的每个星期一次,我们将我们的名字放在这个帽子里,我的还有爸爸的也在。然后我们一个人抽取一个名字,接着就为那个人做一星期的好事。但这里是最难的部分。我们不能告诉任何人我们那个星期抽到了谁的名字,而且我们每个人都要尽可能多的给予那位特殊人士帮助而不要被发现。对我们做的每一件秘密的好事,我们会在婴儿床里放一根稻草。"

"但是如果我抽到了我不喜欢的人呢？"凯丽皱起眉头。

母亲想了一会儿。"也许你可以为你给那个人做的好事放额外大一些

extra fat straws for the good things you do for that person,because they might be harder to do.But just think how much faster the fat straws will fill up our crib.Then on Christmas Eve we'll put Baby Jesus in his little bed,and he'll sleep that night on a mattress made of love.I think he'd like that,don't you?"

"Now,who will build a little crib for us?"she asked.

Since Eric was the oldest,and the only one of the children allowed to use the tools,he marched off to the basement to give it a try. For the next couple of hours,loud banging and sawing noises came from the basement.Then for a long time there were no noises at all.Finally, Eric climbed back up the stairs with the manger in this arms."Here it is,"he grinned."The best crib in the world! And I did it all myself."

For once,everyone agreed:the little manger was the best crib in the world.One leg was an inch too short,of course,and the crib rocked a bit.But it had been built with love—and about a hundred bent nails—and it would certainly last a long time.

"Now we need some straw,"said Mother,and together they headed out to the car to go searching for some in the nearby fields.Surprisingly,no one fought over who was going to sit in the front seat that day as they drove around the countryside,looking for an empty field.At last they spotted a small,vacant patch of land that had been covered with tall grass in the summer.Now,in mid-December,the grass had dried down to yellow stalks that looked just like real straw.

Mother stopped the car and the kids scrambled out to pick handfuls of the tall grass.

"That's enough! "Mother finally laughed,when she saw that the cardboard box in the trunk was almost overflowing. "Remember,it's only a small crib."So home they went,where they spread the straw carefully on a tray Mother had put on the kitchen table.The empty manger was placed gently on top,and the straw hid its one short leg.

"When can we pick names?"shouted the children.

"As soon as Daddy comes home for dinner,"Mother answered.

At the supper table that night,the six names were written on separate pieces of paper,folded up and shuffled around in an old baseball hat.Then the drawing began.

的稻草,因为这会增加事情的难度。但是想一想大一些的稻草会怎样更快地填满我们的婴儿床。然后在圣诞前夕我们就可以把耶稣宝宝放在他的小床里。他将在用爱做成的垫子上酣然入睡。我认为他会喜欢的,你们觉得呢？"

"现在,谁能为我们做一个婴儿床呢？"她问。

因为艾瑞克是最大的,又是孩子们中唯一被允许使用工具的,他走向地下室去一试。在接下来的几小时中,巨大的砰砰声和锯木声从地下室传来。最终艾瑞克从梯子爬了上来,怀里抱着个马槽。"这就是了,"他咧开嘴笑了,"世界上最好的婴儿床！完全是我自己做的！"

这一次,所有的人都同意:这个小马槽是世界上最棒的婴儿床。当然,有一个床腿短了一英寸,而且床有点晃。但是它是用爱建筑成的——大概有一百排的钉子——肯定能够保留很长时间。

"现在我们需要一些稻草,"母亲说,然后他们一起乘车去附近的麦地寻找。令人惊喜的是,当他们在乡下驱车寻找空的麦地时,没有人为谁该坐在前排而争吵。最后他们看见了一小块空地,上面覆盖着夏天时候的蒿草。现在,在12月中旬,这些草都干枯成黄色的秆,看上去像真正的稻草。

母亲停下车,孩子们争先恐后地涌出去捡了大把大把的蒿草。

"足够了！"母亲终于笑了,她看见后备箱里的硬纸板盒子满得几乎溢了出来。"记住,它只是个小婴儿床啊。"当他们回到家后,每个人都把稻草小心地平铺在母亲摆放在厨房餐桌上的盘子里。空空的马槽小心翼翼地被摆放在了顶部,稻草遮住了它短短的一条腿。

"我们什么时候可以选名字！"孩子们喧闹着。

"爸爸一回来吃晚饭就选,"母亲回答。

在那天晚上的餐桌上,6个名字被分别写在了不同的纸上,折叠起来,然后在旧的棒球帽里面充分洗开。接着抓阄开始了。

Kelly picked first and immediately started to giggle.Randi reached into the hat next.Daddy glanced at his scrap of paper and smiled quietly behind his hand.Mother picked out a name,but her face never gave away a clue.Next,little Mike reached into the hat,but since he couldn't read yet,Daddy had to whisper in his ear and tell him which name he had picked.Eric was the last to choose,and as he un-folded his piece of paper a frown crossed his face.But he stuffed the name into his pocket and said nothing.The family was ready to begin.

The week that followed was filled with surprises.It seemed the McDonald house had suddenly been invaded by an army of invisible elves,and good things were happening everywhere.Kelly would walk into her room at bedtime and find her little blue nightgown neatly laid out and her bed turned down.Someone cleaned up the sawdust under the workbench without being asked.The jelly blobs disappeared magically from the kitchen counter after lunch one day while Mother was getting the mail.And every morning,while Eric was brushing his teeth,someone crept quietly into his room and made his bed.It wasn't made perfectly,but it was made.

"Where are my shoes?"asked Daddy one morning.No one seemed to know,but before he left for work,they were back in the closet,all shined up.

Mother noticed other changes during that week,too.The children weren't teasing or fighting as much.An argument would start and then suddenly stop for no apparent reason.Even Eric and Kelly seemed to be getting along better.In fact,all the children wore secret smiles and giggled to themselves at times.

By Sunday,everyone was anxious to pick new names again,and this time there was even more laughter and merriment during the picking process,except for Eric.Once again he unfolded his piece of paper,looked at it,and then stuffed it in his pocket without a word.

Mother noticed,but said nothing.

The second week of the game brought more amazing events.The garbage was taken out without anyone being asked.Someone even did two of Kelly's hard math problems one night when she left her homework out on the table.

The little pile of straw grew higher and softer.With only two

凯丽最先选,立刻就开始窃笑。接着让迪把手伸向帽子。爸爸看了一眼他那张纸片,捂住嘴微笑。母亲选了个名字,不过她丝毫不露声色。接下来,迈克伸向了帽子。但是因为他还不识字,爸爸在他的耳边悄声告诉他抽中的名字。艾瑞克是最后一个抽的,当他打开他的纸片的时候,他的眉头布上了阴云。不过他把名字塞进口袋没说什么。大家准备开始实施计划了。

接下来的一个星期惊喜连连。看上去就像是麦克唐纳家忽然进驻了隐形的小矮人军团,好事处处都在发生。凯丽会在晚上睡觉的时候走进她的房间,发现她的蓝色小睡衣很整洁地摆放着,床也铺好了。有人没有说就把工作台下的木屑清扫干净了。当母亲取邮件回来后就发现厨房台子上的果冻残迹奇迹般地消失了。每天早上,当艾瑞克在刷牙的时候,有人悄悄地潜入他的房间帮他把被子叠好了。虽不是叠得很好,但是叠了。

"我的鞋子呢?"一天早上爸爸问。看上去没有人知道,但是在他上班之前,鞋子已经回到了鞋柜里,发着光亮。

母亲也注意到了这个星期的另外一些变化。孩子们争吵和打架也少了。争论往往一开始,忽然在没有任何理由的情况下就结束了。甚至艾瑞克和凯丽也相处得融洽多了。事实上,所有的孩子都带着神秘的微笑,经常自己就窃笑起来。

星期天,所有的人都再一次急切地要选择新的名字,这一次有更多的笑声和欢闹声,只有艾瑞克没有笑。他再次展开那张纸,看着它,然后一言不发就把它塞进了口袋。母亲注意到了,但也没说什么。

游戏进行到第二周带来了更多让人振奋的事件。垃圾在没有人要求倒的情况下就被带了出去。有人甚至在凯丽把家庭作业丢在桌子上后帮她解决了两道数学难题。

weeks left until Christmas,the children wondered if their homemade bed would be comfortable enough for Baby Jesus.

"Who will be Baby Jesus anyway?"Randi asked on the third Sunday night after they had all picked new names.

"Perhaps we can use one of the dolls,"said Mother. "Why don't you and Mike be in charge of picking out the right one?"

The two younger children ran off to gather up their favorite dolls,but everyone else wanted to help pick Baby Jesus,too.Little Mike dragged his Bozo the Clown rag doll from his room and proudly handed it over,sniffling later when everybody laughed.Soon Eric's well-hugged teddy bear,Bruffles,joined the dolls filling up the couch. Barbie and Ken were there,along with Kermit the Frog,stuffed dogs and lambs,and even a cuddly monkey that Grandma and Grandpa had sent Mike one year.But none of them seemed quite right.

Only an old baby doll,who had been loved almost to pieces, looked like a possibility for their Baby Jesus. "Chatty Baby,"she had once been called,before she stopped chatting forever after too many baths.

"She looks so funny now,"said Randi,and it was true.Once,while playing beauty shop,Kelly had cut her own blonde hair along with Chatty Baby's,giving them both a raggedy crew cut.Kelly's hair had eventually grown back,but Chatty Baby's never had.Now the wisps of blonde hair that stuck out all over the doll's head made her look a little lost and forgotten.But her eyes were still bright blue and she still had a smile on her face,even though her face was smudged here and there by the touch of many chubby little fingers.

"I think she's perfect,"said Mother. "Baby Jesus probably didn't have much hair when he was born either,and I bet he'd like to be represented by a doll who's had so many hugs."

So the decision was made,and the children began to make a new outfit for their Baby Jesus—a little leather vest out of scraps and some cloth diapers.Best of all,Baby Jesus fit perfectly into the little crib,but since it wasn't quite time for him to sleep there yet,he was

小小的稻草堆变得更高更柔软了。剩下两周就要到圣诞节了,孩子们揣测着他们家制的床是否对耶稣宝宝来说足够舒服。

"谁来当耶稣宝宝呢?"让迪在第三个星期天晚上大家抽完名字后问道。

"也许我们可以用一个娃娃,"母亲说,"你和迈克负责选择合适的娃娃吧。"

两个小点的孩子跑去集合起他们最喜欢的娃娃,但是其余的每个人也想帮助选择耶稣宝宝。小迈克从他的房间里拖出小丑破布娃娃博士,然后很骄傲地交给我们,看到每个人都笑起来,他快哭了。很快艾瑞克抱起来很舒服的泰迪熊布鲁夫也加入了娃娃中,沙发都摆满了。芭比和肯也在那儿,还有青蛙可密特,充气狗和充气羊,甚至爷爷奶奶一年前送给迈克的抱着很舒服的猴子也拿出来了。但是他们看上去都不合适。

只有一个旧的布娃娃,已经被太多的爱压得快成了碎片,看上去好像可以当耶稣宝宝。"聊天宝宝",她曾经的名字,但她在经历过太多次的洗澡后已经永远停止了聊天。

"她现在看上去很滑稽,"让迪说,的确如此。曾经有一次在给玩美容店的时候,凯丽把她自己的金发和"聊天宝宝"的金发一起剪了下来,都是潦草粗糙的剪法。凯丽的头发最终长了回来,可是"聊天宝宝"的头发却再也不生长了。现在一根根寸头金发在娃娃的头上竖立着,让她看上去好像被遗弃和淡忘了。但是她的眼睛还是明亮的蓝色,而且她的脸上始终挂着微笑,尽管她的脸已经被很多胖乎乎的小手弄得到处脏兮兮的。

"我认为她是最合适的,"母亲说,"耶稣宝宝大概出生的时候也不会有很多头发,而且我肯定他很愿意让一个拥有很多拥抱的娃娃来做代表。"

当决定做好之后,孩子们开始为耶稣宝宝准备一套新衣服——一个用一些碎布和布尿片做成的小皮背心。最棒的是,小婴儿床对耶稣宝宝来

laid carefully on a shelf in the hall closet to wait for Christmas Eve.

Meanwhile,the pile of straw grew and grew.Every day brought new and different surprises as the secret elves stepped up their activity.The McDonald home was finally filled with Christmas spirit. Only Eric had been unusually quiet since the third week of name picking.

The final Sunday night of name picking was also the night before Christmas Eve.As the family sat around the table waiting for the last set of names to be put in the hat,Mother said,"You've all done a wonderful job.There must be hundreds of straws in our crib—maybe a thousand.You should be so pleased with the bed you've made.But remember,there's still one whole day left.We all have time to do a little more to make the bed even softer before tomorrow night.Let's try."

For the last time,the hat was passed around the table.Little Mike picked out a name,and Daddy whispered it to him,just as he had done every week.Randi unfolded hers carefully under the table,peeked at it and then hunched up her little shoulders,smiling.Kelly reached into the hat and giggled happily when she saw the name.Mother and Daddy each took their turns,too,and then handed the hat with the last name to Eric.But as he unfolded the small scrap of paper and read it, his face pinched up and he suddenly seemed about to cry.Without a word,he ran from the room.

Everyone immediately jumped up from the table,but Mother stopped them."No! Stay where you are,"she said."Let me talk to him alone first."

Just as she reached the top of the stairs,Eric's door banged open. He was trying to pull his coat on with one hand while he carried a small suitcase with the other hand.

"I have to leave,"he said quietly,through his tears. "If I don't,I'll spoil Christmas for everyone! "

"But why?And where are you going?"asked Mother.

"I can sleep in my snow fort for a couple of days.I'll come home right after Christmas.I promise."

Mother started to say something about freezing and snow and no

说非常合适,但是因为现在并不是让他睡在那儿的时间,他被很小心地放在客厅橱柜的架子里等待着圣诞除夕。

与此同时,稻草堆越来越厚。每天当神秘小矮人们做更多的好事,就会带来新的不同的惊喜。麦克唐纳家终于充满了圣诞气氛。只有艾瑞克在第三周的名字抽取后异乎寻常的安静。

最后一次的名字抽取也是在圣诞除夕的前一夜。当家人们围在桌子前等待最后一轮名字放入帽子中,母亲说,"你们都做得非常好。大概有数百根稻草在婴儿床里了——可能是一千根。你们应该为你们做的床而感到满意。但是记住,还剩下最后一天。我们都还有时间在明天晚上之前去多做一点点让床变得更加暖和。让我们试一下吧。"

最后一次,帽子顺着桌子传递着。小迈克取出一个名字,然后爸爸就像每周一样,在他的耳边耳语。让迪小心地在桌下展开她的那张,偷瞄了一眼,耸了一下肩,笑了。凯丽伸向帽子,当她看到名字的时候,笑得很开心。妈妈和爸爸也抽取了他们的一份,然后帽子和里面的最后一个名字传到了艾瑞克手里。但是当他展开这张小的纸片看过后,他的脸拧成一团,他看上去几乎要哭了。他一言不发地冲出了房间。

每个人都立刻从桌旁跳起身来,但是母亲拦住了他们。"不,你们在这,"她说,"让我先单独和他谈谈。"

正当她到达顶层的时候,艾瑞克的门"砰"的一声开了。他正一手试着去穿外套,另一只手拿着个小行李箱。

"我得离开,"他轻声说,带着哭腔。"如果我不走,我会毁了每个人的圣诞!"

"但是为什么？而且你要去哪？"母亲问道。

"我可以在我的雪堡垒里住几天。我在圣诞节后就会回家。我保证。"

母亲开始说一些关于外面很冻,又下雪,没有手套也没有靴子的话,

mittens or boots,but Daddy,who was now standing just behind her, put his hand on her arm and shook his head.The front door closed, and together they watched from the window as the little figure with the sadly slumped shoulders and no hat trudged across the street and sat down on a snowbank near the corner.It was very dark outside,and cold,and a few snow flurries drifted down on the small boy and his suitcase.

"But he'll freeze! "said Mother.

"Give him a few minutes alone,"said Dad quietly. "Then you can talk to him."

The huddled figure was already dusted with white when Mother walked across the street 10 minutes later and sat down beside him on the snowbank.

"What is it,Eric?You've been so good these last few weeks,but I know something's been bothering you since we first started the crib. Can you tell me,honey?"

"Aw,Mom,don't you see?"he sniffled. "I tried so hard,but I can't do it anymore,and now I'm going to wreck Christmas for everyone." With that he burst into sobs and threw himself into his mother's arms.

"But I don't understand,"Mother said,brushing the tears from his face. "What can't you do?And how could you possibly spoil Christmas for us?"

"Mom,"the little boy said through his tears,"you just don't understand.I got Kelly's name *all four weeks*! And I hate Kelly! I can't do one more nice thing for her or I'll die! I tried,Mom.I really did.I sneaked in her room every night and fixed her bed.I even laid out her crummy nightgown.I emptied her wastebasket,and I did some homework for her one night when she was going to the bathroom.Mom,I even let her use my race car one day,but she smashed it right into the wall like always!

"I tried to be nice to her,Mom.Even when she called me a stupid dummy because the crib leg was short,I didn't hit her.And every week,when we picked new names,I thought it would be over.But tonight,when I got her name again,I knew I couldn't do one more nice

但是爸爸,正站在她的身后,把手放在她的手臂上,摇着头。前门关上了,他们看见一个小小的身影,没有戴帽子,跌跌撞撞、步伐艰难地穿过马路,在角落的雪堤处坐下。夜色已经很深了,外面又很冷,几片雪花飘在了小男孩头上和外套上。

"但他会冻坏的!"母亲说。

"让他单独呆几分钟,"爸爸静静地说,"然后你再和他谈谈。"

当母亲10分钟后穿过街道坐在他的身边时,缩成一团的孩子几乎都要被雪覆盖了。

"怎么回事,艾瑞克?你这几个星期表现都那么好,但是我明白我们刚开始实行这个活动时,你就遇到了些问题。你可以告诉我吗,宝贝?"

"啊,妈妈,你没有注意到吗?"他吸着鼻子说。"我很努力地试过了,不过我真的做不下去了,我这样会毁了每个人的圣诞节的,"他扑入母亲的怀中,抽泣起来。

"但我还是不明白,"母亲擦去他脸上的泪水,"你不能够做什么?你怎么可能会毁掉我们的圣诞节呢?

"妈妈,"小男孩带着哭腔说,"你还是不明白。我四周都抽到了凯丽的名字!但是我讨厌凯丽!我不能再为她做一件好事了,否则我会死的!我试过了,妈妈,我真的试过了。我每天晚上都偷偷进她房间帮她铺床。我甚至还把她那破烂的睡衣给摊开放好。我帮她倒垃圾,有一天晚上她去厕所后我还帮她做了家庭作业。妈妈,我有一天甚至让她玩我的赛车,但是她还是像往常一样直直地就往墙上撞去了!

"我试着对她好,妈妈。即使她因为那个短了一条腿的婴儿床骂我傻瓜时我也没揍她。当每周抽新名字的时候,我就想这一切都结束了。但是今天晚上,我又抽到了她的名字,我知道我再也为她做不下去一件好事

thing for her,Mom.I just can't! And tomorrow's Christmas Eve.I'll spoil Christmas for everybody just when we're ready to put Baby Jesus in the crib.Don't you see why I had to leave?"

They sat together quietly for a few minutes,Mother's arm around the small boy's shoulders.Only an occasional sniffle and hiccup broke the silence on the snowbank.

Finally,Mother began to speak softly, "Eric,I'm so proud of you. Every good thing you did should count as double because it was especially hard for you to be nice to Kelly for so long.But you did all those good things anyway,one straw at a time.You gave your love when it wasn't easy to give.Maybe that's what the spirit of Christmas is really all about.If it's too easy to give,maybe we're not really giving much of ourselves after all.The straws you added were probably the most important ones,and you should be proud of yourself."

"Now,how would you like a chance to earn a few easy straws like the rest of us?I still have the name I picked tonight in my pocket, and I haven't looked at it yet.Why don't we switch, just for the last day?It will be our secret."

"That's not cheating?"

"It's not cheating,"Mother smiled.

Together they dried the tears,brushed off the snow and walked back to the house.

The next day the whole family was busy cooking and straightening up the house for Christmas Day,wrapping last-minute presents and trying hard not to burst with excitement.But even with all the activity and eagerness,a flurry of new straws piled up in the crib,and by nightfall it was overflowing.At different times while passing by, each member of the family,big and small,would pause and look at the wonderful pile for a moment,then smile before going on.It was almost time for the tiny crib to be used.But was it soft enough?One straw

might still make a difference.

For that very reason,just before bedtime,Mother tiptoed quietly to Kelly's room to lay out the little blue nightgown and turn down the bed.But she stopped in the doorway,surprised.Someone had already been there.The nightgown was laid neatly across the bed,and a small

了,妈妈,我真的不行!明天就是圣诞除夕。当我们要把耶稣宝宝放进摇篮时,我肯定会弄砸这个圣诞节。你还看不出来我为什么要走吗？"

他们一起静静地坐了几分钟,母亲搂着小男孩,只有偶尔的吸鼻涕和打喷嚏的声音打破着雪堤的寂静。

最后母亲温柔地说,"艾瑞克,我真的为你骄傲。你做的每一件好事都应该算做双份,因为让你对凯丽好这么长时间真的尤其难。你在困难的情况下仍然给予了你的爱。大概这就是圣诞的精神所在吧。如果爱真的很容易就给予了,那么也许我们并没有真正地奉献自我。你添加的稻草大概是最重要的了,你应该为自己感到骄傲。"

"现在,你觉得给你一个像我们大家一样争取几根简单点的稻草的机会怎么样呢？我现在还带着我今天晚上抽到的名字,我还没看呢。我们为什么不换一换呢,只是为了最后一天？这是我们的秘密。"

"那不是作弊吗？"

"不是作弊。"母亲笑了。

于是他们一起擦干眼泪,拍拍身上的雪,回家了。

第二天全家都忙着为圣诞节做菜, 整理房间, 包装着最后的节日礼物,兴奋得都快要炸开了。但是尽管房里处处充满了骚动和热烈的气氛,一些新的稻草又纷纷落在了摇篮里,到晚上都溢了出来。家里大大小小的成员,只要经过,都会驻足欣赏一下这很棒的婴儿床,离开的时候嘴角都会浮现出笑容。快到小摇篮床发挥用途的时候了。但是它已经足够软了吗？再加一根稻草定会让它更加舒适。

正是这个原因,在上床之前,母亲蹑手蹑脚地走进凯丽的房间,准备摊开她蓝色小睡衣,再铺好床。但她惊喜地站在门前。有人已经来过了。睡

red race car rested next to it on the pillow.

　　The last straw was Eric's after all.

Paula McDonald

衣已经整齐地摊开在床上,红色的小赛车静静地躺在枕头的旁边。

　　最后一根稻草还是艾瑞克的。

The Easter Bunny
复活节小兔子

When I was a little girl,every Sunday my family of six would put on their best clothes and go to Sunday School and then church.The kids in elementary school would all meet together to sing songs,and then later divide into groups based on their ages.

One Easter Sunday,all the kids arrived with big eyes and big stories about what the Easter Bunny had brought.While all of the kids shared their stories with delight,one young boy,whom I will call Bobby, sat sullenly.One of the teachers,noticing this,said to him, "And what did the Easter Bunny bring you?"He replied, "My mom locked the door on accident so the Easter Bunny couldn't get inside."

This sounded like a reasonable idea to all of us kids,so we kept on going with the stories.My mom knew the true story,though. Bobby's mom was a single parent,and she suspected that they just couldn't afford the Easter Bunny.

在我还是个小女孩的时候,每个星期天我们家6口人都会穿上最漂亮的衣服去主日学校和教堂。小学的孩子们都将聚在一起唱歌,然后根据年龄大小分成不同的小组。

那是一个复活节的星期天,所有的孩子都来了,个个都睁着大大的眼睛,讲述复活节兔子送给他们的礼物的长长的故事。正当他们兴高采烈地和其他人分享的时候,一个叫鲍比的小男孩却坐在那闷闷不乐一言不发。其中一位老师看到这一幕就问:"你的复活节兔子送你什么了?"他回答道:"我妈妈不小心把门锁上了,复活节兔子没办法进来。"

他的回答在我们这些小孩子听起来很合乎常理,于是大家继续讲着故事。可是我妈妈知道真实的情况。鲍比的妈妈是单亲妈妈,所以她怀疑

After Sunday School was over,everyone went off to church.When my dad came to meet us my mom announced that we were going home instead.At home,she explained that to make Bobby feel better, we were going to pretend to be the Easter Bunny and make a basket of goodies for him and leave it at church.We all donated some of our candies to the basket,and headed back up to church.There,mom unzipped his coat,hung the basket over the hanger,and zipped up the coat and attached a note.

Dear Bobby,
I'm sorry I missed your house last night.Happy Easter.
Love,
The Easter Bunny

by Beth H.Arbogast

他们是没能力买这些东西的。

主日学校放学以后,所有人都去了教堂。当爸爸来接我们的时候,妈妈却宣布决定我们全部回家,不去教堂了。回到家,妈妈提议我们应该为鲍比做点什么让他好受点。我们打算假装成复活节兔子,为他做一个花篮放在教堂。我们兄妹几个纷纷拿出一些糖果放在篮子里把它挂在教堂的后面。妈妈解开鲍比的外套把篮子挂在衣架上,然后把外套的拉锁拉上并且系上一个便签。

亲爱的鲍比,
很抱歉,昨夜我漏掉去你家了。祝你复活节快乐。
爱你的
复活节兔子

译者注:在西方,复活节是一年中最重要的宗教节日之一。节日源自耶稣被钉死于十字架之后又复活了。但孩子们在这一天兴奋不已却是出于另外的原因：他们会从亲朋好友那里得到一些复活节小礼物。孩子们的这一天，是从寻找父母事先藏好的复活节篮子开始的。按照传统，在被装饰得五颜六色的篮子里，还会在小玩具旁边放上复活节彩蛋和复活节兔子。这一风俗可以追溯到一个古老的日耳曼人的传统。复活节是在公元4世纪传入德国的，为了使新的教会节日在日耳曼人当中得到更广泛的传播，教父就把它和当时传统的非基督教的日耳曼风俗结合起来。而且人们在春季的开始来庆祝这一节日，以此来祈求一个丰收年。兔子象征着子孙后代的繁衍。因为兔子的繁殖能力比较强，所以人们经常用兔子来作象征。还有鸡蛋，它在很多文化中同样是生命及生命之源的象征。

The Eyes of Tex
特克斯的眼睛

Eric Seal thought the scrawny puppy at his feet was perhaps five weeks old.Sometime during the night,the little mixed-breed female had been dumped at the Seals' front gate.

"Before you ask,"he told Jeffrey,his wife,"the answer is an absolute *no*! We are not going to keep it.We don't need another dog.When and if we do,we'll get a purebred."

As though she hadn't heard him,his wife sweetly asked,"What kind do you think it is?"

Eric shook his head. "It's hard to tell.From her color markings and the way she holds her ears in a half-lop,I'd say she's part German shepherd."

"We can't just turn her away,"Jeffrey pleaded. "I'll feed her and get her cleaned up.Then we'll find a home for her."

Standing between them,the puppy seemed to sense that her fate was being decided.Her tail wagged tentatively as she looked from one to the other.Eric noticed that although her ribs showed through a dull coat,her eyes were bright and animated.

Finally,he shrugged his shoulders. "Okay,if you want to fool with her,go ahead.But let's get one thing straight:We don't need a Heinz-57 mongrel."

The puppy nestled comfortably in Jeffrey's arms as they walked toward the house. "One other thing,"Eric continued. "Let's wait a few days to put her in the pen with Tex.We don't want Tex exposed to anything.He has all the troubles he can handle."

Tex,the six-year-old cattle dog the Seals had raised from a puppy, was unusually amiable for a blue-heeler,a breed established by ranchers in Australia.So,although he already shared his doghouse with a yellow cat,soon Tex happily moved over and made room for the new puppy the Seals called Heinz.

Not long before Heinz showed up,the Seals had noticed that Tex

埃里克·西尔想,他膝下这条骨瘦如柴的小狗也许有5个星期大了。半夜时分,有人把这只混血母狗扔在西尔家门口前。

"在你提问之前,"埃里克对他妻子杰弗里说,"我敢肯定回答绝对是'不'！我们不打算收留它。我们不需要再养一条狗。如果真要养的话,就养一只纯种的。"

好像他妻子没听见他说什么,甜甜地问:"你知道这条狗是哪一种类型的吗?"

埃里克摇摇头。"这一时很难说出来。从颜色斑点和它半耷拉着的耳朵的样子看,我想它有德国牧羊犬的血统。"

"我们不能就这么把它拒之门外,"杰弗里恳求道,"我来喂它,把它洗干净。然后给它找个家。"

小狗站在他们俩中间,似乎意识到它的命运将被确定下来了。它东瞧瞧,西看看,试探性地摇动着尾巴。埃里克注意到小狗没有光泽的毛下面虽是骨瘦如柴,可它那双眼睛明亮的炯炯有神。

最后埃里克耸耸肩说:"那好吧,如果你想摆弄它,就随你吧。不过有一点要说清楚:我们不需要海因茨杂种狗。"

他们朝房子走去,那小狗舒服地窝在杰弗怀里,"埃里克继续说道,"还有一件事,等几天再让它进特克斯的窝。咱们不要给特克斯添新的麻烦,它吃的苦已经够多了。"

特克斯是条西尔夫妇从小养大的牧牛狗,如今已经6岁。它是澳大利亚牧场主培育的一种狗种,特别惹人喜欢。尽管它的狗窝里已经有了一只黄猫,它还是高兴地腾出些地方让给这只被西尔夫妇称作海因茨的狗。

就在海因茨出现前不久,西尔夫妇已注意到特克斯好像正在失去

appeared to be losing his eyesight.Their veterinarian said he thought the dog had cataracts that might be surgically removed.

But when they brought Tex to a specialist in Dallas,he determined that the dog's poor eyesight was only partially due to cataracts.He made an appointment for Tex at the local college's veterinary laboratory.

Doctors there determined that Tex was already blind.They explained that no medical or surgical procedure could have halted or delayed Tex's progressive loss of vision.

As they talked on their way home,the Seals realized that over the last few months,they had watched Tex cope with his blindness.Now they understood why Tex sometimes missed a gate opening or bumped his nose on the chain-link fence.And why he usually stayed on the gravel walkways traveling to and from the house.If he wan dered off,he quartered back and forth until he was on the gravel again.

While the couple had been preoccupied with Tex's troubles,Heinz had grown plump and frisky,and her dark brown-and-black coat glowed with health.

It was soon obvious that the little German shepherd crossbreed would be a large dog—too large to continue sharing a doghouse with Tex and the yellow cat.One weekend,the Seals built another doghouse next to the one the dogs had shared.

It was then they recognized that what they had assumed was puppy playfulness—Heinz's pushing and tugging at Tex while romping with him—actually had a purpose.Without any training or coaching, Heinz had become Tex's "seeing eye" dog.

Each evening when the dogs settled in for the night,Heinz gently took Tex's nose in her mouth and led him into his house.In the morning,she got him up and guided him out of the house again.

When the two dogs approached a gate,Heinz used her shoulder to guide Tex through.When they ran along the fence surrounding their pen,Heinz placed herself between Tex and the wire.

"On sunny days,Tex sleeps stretched out on the driveway as-

视力,他们请的兽医认为这只狗患了白内障,也许可以动手术把白内障除掉。

但当西尔夫妇带着特克斯到达拉斯兽医专科医院检查时，专家诊断白内障只是造成视力衰弱的部分原因。他为特克斯在当地一个学院的兽医学实验室做了预约。

实验室的医生们断定特克斯早已丧失视力，并解释说任何医药或手术措施都无法终止或延缓它的视力衰弱的进程。

回家的路上，西尔夫妇说着说着，不禁想起在过去几个月里，他们实际看到特克斯是如何应付自己的失明状况的。现在他们终于明白了为什么它有时候没有赶上正在开启的门，或把自己的鼻子撞到了金属防护网上，为什么它出来进去总是沿着石子道走；一旦走偏，它就摸索着直至再走回石子道上来。

西尔夫妇一直忙着特克斯失明的事，不知不觉中海因茨已长得肥肥胖胖、活蹦乱跳的，深棕黑色的毛呈现出健康的光泽。

没多久就看得出这只小德国杂种牧羊狗会长成一条大狗，大到不能再和特克斯及黄猫共同居住在一间狗屋里了。一个周末，西尔夫妇在原来的狗屋旁又建了间新屋。

就在这个时候，他们才明白，原先认为海因茨跟特克斯玩闹时推推搡搡，只是小狗的嬉戏顽皮，其实那是有目的性的。没有经过任何训练或辅导，海因茨成了特克斯的导盲犬。

每天傍晚两只狗要进狗屋过夜时，海因茨就用它的嘴轻轻咬住特克斯的鼻子，领着它进屋。早上海因茨叫它起来，再领着它出屋。

两只狗来到门前时，海因茨用肩头引着特克斯通过大门，要是它们沿着狗圈围栏跑，海因茨就跑在特克斯和围栏之间，用自己的身体挡着。

"阳光和煦的日子，特克斯四条腿伸开睡在柏油车道上，"杰弗里说

phalt,"says Jeffrey. "If a car approaches,Heinz will nudge him awake and guide him out of danger."

"Any number of times we've seen Heinz push Tex aside to get him out of the horses' way.What we didn't understand at first was how the two could run side by side,dashing full speed across the pasture.Then one day,the dogs accompanied me while I exercised my horse,and I heard Heinz 'talking'—she was making a series of soft grunts to keep Tex on course beside her."

The Seals were awed.Without any training,the young dog had devised whatever means were necessary to help,guide and protect her blind companion.It was clear that Heinz shared more than her eyes with Tex;she shared her heart.

Honzie L.Rodgers

道。"有车来了,海因茨就用蹄子把它轻轻推醒,引着它脱离危险。"

"不知多少次我们看见海因茨把特克斯从马腿边推开。开始我们不明白为什么它们俩能在牧场上并排飞跑。后来有一天,两只狗陪着我练习骑马,我听见海因茨在'说话',原来它在连续发出轻轻的呼噜声,指引特克斯在它旁边。"

西尔夫妇对海因茨充满了敬畏。没有经过任何训练,这条年轻的狗想出各种必要的方法帮助、引导并保护着失明的伙伴。显而易见,与其说特克斯分享的是海因茨的眼睛,不如说它分享更多的是海因茨的一颗心。

The Tablecloth
台布

A young minister had been called to serve at an old church that at one time had been a magnificent edifice in a wealthy part of town. Now the area was in a state of decline and the church was in bad shape.Nevertheless,the pastor and his wife were thrilled with the church and believed they could restore it to its former magnificence.

When the minister took charge of the church early in October 1948,he and his wife immediately went to work painting,repairing and attempting to restore it.Their goal was to have the old edifice looking its best for Christmas Eve services.

Just two days before Christmas,however,a storm swept through the area,dumping more than an inch of rain.The roof of the old church sprung a leak just behind the altar.The plaster soaked up the water as if it were a sponge and then crumbled,leaving a gaping hole in the wall.

一位年轻的牧师在一座古老的教堂里工作,这座教堂曾一度辉煌,它就坐落在小城的富庶区。而今,这里渐渐萧条,教堂也破旧不堪。即便如此,牧师和他的妻子仍然充满信心,因为他们相信有朝一日会令教堂重现辉煌。

1948年10月的上旬,牧师接管了这座教堂。很快这对夫妇就着手教堂的修缮工作,力图恢复旧貌。打算在平安夜礼拜前,让这座破旧的教堂焕然一新。

然而就在圣诞节的前两天,一场暴风雨席卷了这个地区,降下一英寸多的雨水。老教堂圣坛后面的屋顶,突然开了一道裂缝。石灰墙如同一块海绵,吸干了漏下的雨水,然后就软化了,在墙上留下了一道缝隙。

Dejected,the pastor and his wife looked at the defaced wall. There was obviously no chance to repair the damage before Christmas.Nearly three months of hard work had been washed way.Yet the young couple accepted the damage as God's will and set about cleaning up the damp debris.

It was a depressed minister and his wife who attended a benefit auction for the church youth group that afternoon.One of the items put of for bid was an old gold-and-ivory-colored lace tablecloth,nearly fifteen feet long.

Seized with an inspiration,the pastor was the high bidder at $6.50.His idea was to hang the orange cloth behind the altar to cover the ragged hole in the wall.

On the day before Christmas,snowflakes mingled with the howling wind.As the pastor unlocked the church doors,he noticed an older woman standing at the nearby bus stop.He knew the bus wouldn't be there for at least half an hour,so he invited her inside to keep warm.

She wasn't from the neighborhood,she explained.She had been in the area to be interviewed for a job as a governess to the children of a well-known wealthy family.She had been a war refugee,her English was poor and she didn't get the job.

Head bowed in prayer,she sat in the pew near the back of the church.She paid no attention to the pastor,who was hanging the tablecloth across the unsightly hole.When the woman looked up and saw the cloth she rushed to the altar.

"It's mine! "she exclaimed."It's my banquet cloth! "

Excitedly she told the surprised minister its history and even showed him her initials embroidered in one corner.

She and her husband had lived in Vienna,Austria,and had opposed the Nazis before the Second World War.They decided to flee to Switzerland,but her husband said they must go separately.She left first.Later she heard that he had died in a concentration camp.

Touched by her story,the minister insisted that she take the cloth.She thought about it for a moment but said no,she didn't need it any longer,and it did look pretty hanging behind the altar.Then she said good-bye and left.

In the candlelight of the Christmas Eve services,the tablecloth

牧师夫妇沮丧地望着污损的墙面，很显然要在圣诞节前修好它已经没有时间了。将近三个月的辛劳毁于一旦,但他们认为这是上帝的安排,于是着手清理那些湿淋淋的粉渣。

那天下午,这对沮丧的夫妇参加了为教堂青年举办的公益拍卖活动。其中的拍卖品之一是一块金黄色的镶着象牙边的台布,几乎有15英尺长。

牧师灵机一动,打算就用这块橙色的台布悬挂在圣坛后面,来遮住墙上的那个破洞。他叫出6.5美元的最高价,结果拍下了。

圣诞节前一天,雪花伴随着呼号的寒风飘落下来。当牧师去教堂开门的时候,他发现一位老太太站在附近的公交站牌下。牧师知道公交车至少在半小时以后才来,于是他就邀请老太太进屋来避避风雪。

老太太说自己不住在这个区,因为附近一大户人家聘请家庭教师,她是来参加面试的。自己是战争难民加上英语又差,结果没得到这份工作。

她坐在教堂靠后面的长椅上,低头默祷。她没在意牧师,他正在用那块台布遮住那个不雅的破洞。当老妇人抬起头看到这块布时,便冲向圣坛。

"这是我的!"她大呼。"这是我的宴会台布!"

这一举动让牧师惊呆了, 接着她万分激动地向牧师道出了台布的故事,甚至还指出了台布一角的刺绣。

她和丈夫原先住在奥地利维也纳,二战前他们反对纳粹统治。后来决定逃亡到瑞士,但她丈夫说必须分开走。于是她先走了,再后来听说丈夫死于集中营。

牧师被她的故事深深感动了,坚持要她带走这块台布。她想了一会儿却说不用了,她已不再需要它了,而且它挂在圣坛后面也的确漂亮。然后她告辞离开了。

looked even more magnificent.The white lace seemed dazzling in the flickering light of the candles,and the golden threads woven through it were like the brilliant rays of a new dawn.

As members of the congregation left the church,they complimented the pastor on the services and on how beautiful the church looked.

One older gentlemen lingered,admiring the tablecloth,and as he was leaving he said to the minister:

"It's strange.Many years ago my wife—God rest her—and I owned such a tablecloth.She used it only on very special occasions. But we lived in Vienna then."

The night air was freezing,but the goosebumps on the pastor's skin weren't caused by the weather.As calmly as he could,he told the man about the woman who had been to the church that very afternoon.

"Can it be,"gasped the old man,tears streaming down his cheeks, "that she is alive?How can I find her?"

The pastor remembered the name of the family who had interviewed the woman.With the trembling old man at his side,he telephoned the family and learned her name and address.

In the pastor's old car they drove to her home on the other side of town.Together they knocked on her apartment door.When she opened it,the pastor witnessed the tearful,joyful and thrilling reunion of husband and wife.

Some people would call it an extremely lucky chance happening, the result of a hole in the church wall,an old tablecloth,a pastor's ingenuity in solving a problem and so on.But the combination of events was far too complex for it to have been merely"coincidence."

If one link in the fragile chain of events had been broken,the husband and wife might never have found each other.If the rain hadn't come,if the church roof hadn't leaked,if the pastor had decided not to go to the auction,if the woman hadn't been looking for a job or standing on that corner at just the right time... the list of ifs is virtually endless.

It was simply God's will.And,as it has been said many times,He works in mysterious ways.

在平安夜礼拜的烛光中,这块台布熠熠发光。白色的镶边在烛光的映射下令人眼花缭乱,穿梭其中的金线如同一道道黎明的曙光。

当集会的人们离开教堂时, 他们对牧师的安排和对教堂的布置称赞不已。

一位年迈的绅士在台布前来回徘徊, 羡慕地望着它, 当他准备离开时,他对牧师说:

"真是不可思议,许多年以前我和我已逝的妻子也有一块和这一样的台布。她只在一些特殊的场合用用,那时我们住在维也纳。"

夜晚的气温正在下降, 但牧师却丝毫感觉不到寒意。他努力保持镇定,他告诉绅士就在那天下午,那位太太曾到过这座教堂。

"真的?她还活着?怎么才能找到她?"老人急喘着,激动得泪流满面。

牧师想起老太太曾去面试过的那户人家,于是牧师拨通了那家的号码。得知了老太太现在的姓名和住址,老人在旁激动得颤抖不已。

坐着牧师的旧车,他们一道驶向住在小城另一边的老太太住所。他们敲了敲老太太的门,结果真的开了。牧师目睹了这场悲喜交加的重逢,既有欢喜,又有泪水。

有人会说这是一次极幸运的巧合,教堂破洞的出现,一块旧台布以及牧师解决问题的机智等。一连串事件的组合真是太复杂了,几乎是一种巧合。

如果这件事的整个链条上任何一条断了, 这对夫妇可能永远也不会相见。如果没有那场大雨,如果屋顶不漏雨,如果牧师不去那次拍卖会,如果那位老太太不是一直在寻找一份工作, 如果她当时不站在那个角落——这样的如果是无休无止的。

这只是上帝的意愿,这样的话已经说过多次了。他总是用一种神秘的方式安排着他的子民的命运。

生命的彩虹

129

Steal What?
盗什么？

This story took place several years ago,when our boys were about eight years old.It was the first game of the season,and the first game in which the boys began pitching.I went out to discuss ground rules with the umpire and realized that this was also the first year that the boys could steal bases.Unfortunately,we had not gone over this in practice.So I hurried back to the dugout,gathered my players and proceeded to go over the rules.

As I got to the subject of stealing bases,I announced enthusiastically, "And this year we get to steal! "The news caused the boys to erupt into yelling and cheering.Their response left me thinking positively that this might all work out okay after all.Then the cheers died down,and as our team was about to take the field,one player loudly exclaimed,"Steal what?! "I let out a groan as I realized that the ques-

故事发生在好几年前,那时棒球队的男孩子们约摸只有8岁光景。记得那是当季的第一场比赛,男孩们刚开始学习投球,我去找裁判员讨论比赛程序,才知道这一年允许球员盗垒。遗憾的是,我们队还从来没有实际操练过这一项。我匆匆赶回棒球队员休息的地方,召集队员,研究比赛规则,商量对策。

谈到"盗垒"这一新规则时, 我故意高声宣布:"今年我们可以盗垒了! "(译者注:盗垒就是在一次投球后,没有击球员、游击手、传球手或外野手的帮助而安全跑入另一垒)。孩子们欢呼雀跃起来,看到他们的反应,我乐观地想:也许没什么问题。可惜"好景不长",正当我们队准备开始比赛时,有人大声地问:"我们要去盗什么东西?!"我长叹一声,要知道,问这

tion had come from my son!

Cary McMahon

话的是我儿子!

When Snowball Melted
当雪球融化时

Hope is the thing with feathers
That perches in the soul.
And sings the tune
Without the words,
And never stops at all.

Emily Dickinson

希望是鸟儿，
在人们心灵栖居，
唱着无词的歌儿，
永无止息。

爱米莉·狄更生

Lovebirds. That's what all our friends called us when we first married.

I guess Don and I deserved it. Money was tight because we were both full-time students, working to pay our way through school. Sometimes we'd have to save up days just for an ice cream cone. Still, our tiny, drab apartment seemed like paradise. Love does that, you know.

Anyway, the more we heard the term "lovebirds," the more we thought about birds. And one day we started saving up for a couple of lovebirds of our own: the feathery kind. We knew we couldn't afford to buy both birds *and* a nice cage, so in his spare moments, Don made the cage himself.

We set our cage in front of a shaded window. Then we waited

until the crumpled envelope marked "lovebirds"was full of bills and spare change.At last the day came when we were able to walk down to our local pet store to"adopt"some additions to our little family.

We'd had our hearts set on parakeets.But the minute we heard the canaries singing,we changed our minds.Selecting a lively yellow male and a sweet white female,we named the youngsters Sunshine and Snowball.

Because of our exhausting schedules,we didn't get to spend too much time with our new friends,but we loved having them greet us each evening with bursts of song.And they seemed blissfully happy with each other.

"情爱鸟",我们刚结婚时朋友们就这么称呼我们的。

我想我和唐对这个名字受之无愧。我们两人都是全日制学生,靠打工挣学费,所以手头总是很紧。有时为了能买个冰激凌蛋卷我们就要攒好几天的钱。即便如此,我们那个狭小、简陋的公寓房看起来还像天堂一般。很显然,这是真爱使然。

不管怎么说,我们越是听了"情爱鸟"这个称呼,就越是想到了小鸟。我们开始攒钱给自己买一对情侣鹦鹉,羽毛柔软的那种。我们知道我们没钱既买鹦鹉又买个像样子的鸟笼,所以唐就利用业余时间自己动手做了个鸟笼。

我们把鸟笼放在一个阴凉的窗下,然后等待着有一天那个皱巴巴的、上面写着"情侣鹦鹉"的信封里面装满了纸币和多余的硬币。到当地的宠物店为我们的小家"领养"新成员的这一天终于到来了。

本来一心想养一对长尾小鹦鹉。可是一听到那金丝雀的歌声,我们既定的主意就改了。我们挑选了一只特明亮跳跃的黄色雄鸟和一只乳白色的雌鸟,给这对小鸟取名为"阳光"和"雪球"。

由于我们每天都忙得令人疲乏不堪,没有太多的时间陪这两个新朋友,但我们爱听它们用美妙的歌声每晚迎接我们归来。它们看上去也相处得非常幸福愉快。

Time passed,and when our young lovebirds finally seemed mature enough to start a family of their own,we went ahead and prepared a nest area and lots of nesting material for them.

Sure enough,one day they began to find the idea very appealing. Snowball was a very exacting supervisor in designing and decorating their nest just so,while Sunshine,his face aglow with love,bent over backward to put everything just where she ordered.

Then one day an egg appeared.How they sang! And a few weeks later when a tiny chick hatched,their happiness seemed to know no bounds.I don't know how it happened genetically,but that baby canary was bright orange.So right off we named him Punkinhead.

The sunny days passed.How proud all of us were when our fledgling tottered out of the nest onto a real grown-up perch!

Then one day,Punkinhead suddenly plunged headlong from his perch to the bottom of the cage.The tiny orange bird just lay there. Both parents and I rushed to his rescue.

But he was dead.Just like that.Whether he'd had a heart attack before he fell or broke his neck in the fall,I'll never know.But Punkinhead was gone.

Though both parents grieved,his little mother was inconsolable. She refused to let either Sunshine or me get near that pitiful little body.Instead of the joyful melodies I usually heard from Snowball, now she gave only the most excruciating cries and moans.Her heart, joy and will seemed completely melted by her sorrow.

Poor Sunshine didn't know what to make of it.He kept trying to push Snowball away from her sad station,but she refused to budge. Instead,over and over she kept trying to revive her adored child.

Finally Sunshine seemed to work out a plan.He convinced her to fly up and eat some seeds every so often,while he stood duty in her place.Then each time she left,he'd quietly place one piece of nesting straw over Punkinhead's body.Just one.But in a few days,piece by piece,it was completely covered over.

At first Snowball seemed disoriented when she looked around,

时间一天天过去,这对恩爱小鸟终于长大成熟可以给自己成个家了。我们提早在鸟笼里给它们准备了一个做窝的位置和许多做窝的材料。

果然,有一天它们开始觉得这个主意很吸引人。在设计和装饰爱巢方面,"雪球"俨然像个严谨的主管,而"阳光"则满脸兴奋地按"雪球"的指令不遗余力地把东西放好。

这之后的一天,一只鸟蛋出现了。"阳光"和"雪球"高兴地欢唱着!几个星期后,一只小鸟破壳而出。它们欣喜万分。我并不清楚遗传的方式,但这只小金丝雀却是明亮的橙黄色。我们马上想到了"南瓜头"这个名字。

阳光灿烂的日子一天天过去。看着我们的小家伙羽毛日渐丰满并开始蹒跚地走出它的小巢爬到为成年鸟准备的栖木上时,我们是多么的为它骄傲!

后来有一天,"南瓜头"突然从栖木上一头栽到了鸟笼子的底儿上。这只橙黄色的小鸟躺在那儿一动不动。它的父母和我都立即冲过去抢救。

然而,它却死了,就那样地死了。我永远都无法知晓,它到底是怎么死的;是它突发了心脏病摔下来了,还是在摔下来时折断了脖子?不管怎么样,"南瓜头"永远地离去了。

鸟爸爸和鸟妈妈都很难过,小鸟妈妈更悲伤欲绝。它拒绝"阳光"或是我接近那个可怜的小肉体。我听不到"雪球"像以前那样欢快地鸣唱,听到的只是它的悲叫与哀鸣。它的心、它的欢快和它的希望好像完全都被它的悲哀击碎了。

可怜的"阳光"不知所措,它一次又一次试着想帮"雪球"从悲伤之地推开,但"雪球"拒绝挪动,绝不离开一步。而它一次又一次地想把爱子救活。

最后,"阳光"似乎是想出了一个办法,它成功地说服"雪球"不时地飞到上面的栖木去吃些东西,而它替"雪球"陪在死去的小宝宝身边。于是每当"雪球"飞走,它都悄悄地叼一根造窝的草盖在"南瓜头"身上,每次仅仅一根。这样过了几天,一根根地,"南瓜头"的尸体就全被覆盖住了。

but she didn't try to uncover the chick.Instead,she flew up to her normal perch and stayed there.Then I was able to quietly reach in and remove the little body,straw shroud and all.

After that,Sunshine spent all his time consoling Snowball.Eventually she started making normal sounds,and then one day,her sorrow finally melted and she sang again.

I don't know if Snowball ever realized the quiet labor of love and healing Sunshine had done for her.But they remained joyously devoted for as long as they both lived.Love does that,you know.

Especially to lovebirds.

Bonnie Compton Hanson

开始,"雪球"四处张望,好像失去了方向,但她并没有试图揭开盖在"南瓜头"身上的草,而是飞到它惯用的栖木上呆在那儿。这样我就可以悄悄地走近鸟笼挪走"南瓜头"的尸体和裹在它身上的稻草。

在那之后,"阳光"把它所有的时间都花在安慰"雪球"上,"雪球"终于开始恢复了原来的声音。后来有一天,"雪球"的悲怆消融了,它又唱起歌来。

我不知道"雪球"是否意识到"阳光"为使它从悲伤中恢复过来而悄悄付出的爱和辛劳。但它们终生相亲相爱,快乐无比。很清楚,这全凭借了爱的力量。

对于"情爱鸟"更是如此。

The Good Side of Fear
害怕也有好的一面

I had the chance to sit down at Jack Murphy Stadium in San Diego with Joe Montana before he went onto the field with the San Francisco 49ers against Denver in Super Bowl XXIV (1989).We didn't know it then,but this would be Joe's last Super Bowl,his fourth championship and yet another high point in one of the most remarkable careers not just in pro football,but in all of sports.

Joe seemed restless.He had already won everything there is in this game—the respect of teammates and opponents,coaches and owners,and especially the fans—plus all the awards:multiple League Most Valuable Player awards (MVPs),Super Bowls and Super Bowl MVPs.

I said,"Joe,you can't possibly be scared."

What he said to me is,I believe,the key to his success and the reason I consider him the greatest quarterback of all time.He said,"If

那是1989年的美国橄榄球超级杯大赛,在圣地亚哥杰克·莫菲体育场旧金山淘金者队对阵丹佛队,开赛前,我有幸和乔·蒙唐纳坐在一起。当时我并不知道,这将是乔最后一次参加"超级杯",也是他运动生涯里的第四次夺冠,这样的成绩不仅是橄榄球运动史上新一轮的高潮,对于任何体育运动事业,都堪称"凤毛麟角"。

乔一直锐意进取,事业的成功为他赢得了一切:队友和对手们的尊敬、教练员和经理人的赏识、球迷们的爱戴。除此之外,他更是获奖无数:联队最具价值球员奖、"超级杯"赛大奖以及"超级杯"最具价值球员奖。

我说:"乔,你应该从来没有感觉到害怕。"

"如果你一点也不害怕失败,那么失败就不会有存在的价值了。"乔的

you're not afraid of losing,then losing means nothing."

Every time Joe Montana stepped on the field,he was scared.That element of fear kept him sharp through his entire career.If we want to be at our best,we need that same element of fear burning inside of us.It sharpens the focus,keeps the edge.

There isn't a day that goes by that I don't remember what Joe said,realizing the truth of it.It has helped me.I know it will surely help you.

Joe Theismann

回答让我相信这就是他成功的秘笈，也是我深信他会是橄榄球运动史上最伟大的四分卫的原因。

每次踏入赛场,乔·蒙唐纳都感到害怕,正是这种紧张不安让他在整个职业生涯里保持敏锐、机警,如果我们也想做到最好,我们同样也须"惴惴不安",只有这样才能养精蓄锐。

这么多年过去,我从未忘记乔的话,时常细细品味,体会其中真谛,它曾启发过我,相信也会对你们大有裨益。

25

The Mitzvah
善哉善哉

It was fall 1945,and I returned to Vienna with the first American occupation troops.I had been there three months earlier as an interpreter of German for a special mission assigned to negotiate the division of the city into four allied zones,similar to what had been done in Berlin.I was fluent in German because,only six years earlier,I had emigrated to the United States from Berlin.As soon as I became eligible,I enlisted in the U.S. Army to serve my new country and was proud to wear its uniform.

One Friday night,feeling somewhat homesick,I made my way to the only remaining synagogue in Vienna to attend services.The crowd there was a pitiful sight,about fifty men and women,thin and poorly dressed.They spoke accented Yiddish,and I surmised that they were the remnants of thriving Jewish communities across Europe,now thrown together in this one place and cut off from the rest of the world.When they spotted my American uniform,they all crowded

那是1945年的秋天,我跟随首支美国占领部队返回越南。3个月前,我还在越南,当时那儿正有一场谈判,旨在将这所城市划分为4个占领区,就像柏林那样,我是这个特别任务的德语翻译。6年前才从柏林移居美国的我,讲着一口流利的德语,入伍资格一具备,我便迫不及待地参了军,效力美国。能穿上美军制服我很自豪。

一个星期五的晚上,感觉有点想家,我便去了越南唯一残存的犹太教堂做礼拜,到了那儿,场面很是凄凉,50个左右的男男女女,全都面黄肌瘦,衣衫褴褛,他们说着带口音的依第语,我猜想,他们应该是从欧洲逃难幸存下来的犹太人,与外部世界失去了联系。当他们看到我的美军制服

生命的彩虹

139

around me to see a friendly soldier in a synagogue.To their surprise,I was able to converse with them in fluent Yiddish.

As we talked,I could tell my initial assessment was correct.These people were survivors of the Holocaust who had gathered at the synagogue to see if they could find someone,anyone,who might know of a relative or friend who had also survived.Because there was no civilian mail service from Austria to the rest of the world,these gatherings were the only way the survivors could hope to hear news of their families.

One of the men timidly asked me if I would be kind enough to send a message to a relative in England that he was still alive.I knew that military mail service was not to be used for civilian letters,but how could I say no?These people,who had literally been through a living hell,needed to let worried relatives know they had survived. When I agreed,everyone wanted to send a message.

Fifty messages were a lot more than one: I had to think quickly. Standing back,I announced that I would return to services the following Friday night and accept short messages written in English, German or Yiddish and submitted in an unsealed envelope.If the letters met those requirements,I would send them by military mail.

The following week,as promised,I once again made my way to the synagogue.As I opened the door,I was shocked.The place was packed,full of people who rushed up to me,thrusting their envelopes toward me.There were so many that I had to ask someone to find me a box in which to store them.I spent the next week checking each message for security reasons,making sure it contained only the promised announcement.Then I sent mail all over the world.I felt wonderful to know that this would probably be the first news to most of these relatives that one of their loved ones had survived the horrors of the Holocaust.A good deed,I thought,a little "mitzvah."

About a month passed.The whole thing had started to fade from my mind when the military "mailboy" suddenly stumbled into my office,laden with several sacks of packages.

"What's going on?"he demanded.The parcels he set on the floor

时，便全凑上前来细细打量我这个还算和善的美军战士。我能用一口流利的依第语与他们交谈，这让他们很惊讶。

随着谈话的深入，我发现先前对于这群人的判断是正确的，这群犹太人是大屠杀的幸存者，他们聚集到这个犹太教堂是为了寻找任何一个可能知道他们亲人或者朋友是否还活着的人。由于从奥地利往外已经没有了公共邮政服务，聚会成了这些思亲心切的难民获得家人消息的唯一途径。

一个男人小心翼翼地问我是否能行个好，帮他给英国的一个亲戚带个信，告诉他们他还活着，军用邮政是不能寄民信的，这我当然清楚，可我怎么忍心拒绝？这些受尽折磨的犹太难民，渴望让自己担惊受怕的亲人知道他们已虎口脱险。我同意了。马上所有的人都想寄信，50封民信可不是个小数目，我必须很快考虑清楚。于是我向后退了几步，大声宣布：下个星期五晚上，我还会来做礼拜，到时来收信。

信件得用英文、德文和依第文书写，不能太长也不能封缄，只要符合这样的要求，我会通过军用邮政把它们寄出去。

下个周末到了，我按承诺，再次前往教堂，推开门的一刹那，我被震住了，教堂里挤得水泄不通，人们全都向我涌来，争相把信交给我。由于信件实在太多，我不得不让人帮我找个装信的箱子。接下来的那一整个星期，出于安全原因，我得给每一封信件做检查以确保它们符合规定，随后便将它们发往世界各地。一想到这些信件很有可能第一次让亲人们知晓自己牵挂的人侥幸逃过大屠杀还活在人世，我便深感欣慰。是件好事，我暗自寻思，"善哉善哉"。

一个月过去了，我差不多快忘了这事，突然有天部队里的"邮递员"扛着几大麻袋包裹闯进我办公室。

"这是怎么一回事？"他盘问道，地上几麻袋的包裹来自世界各地，是

came from everywhere,addressed to the survivors I had met in the synagogue,in care of me,Corporal Arnold Geier.I had not expected this result.What was I supposed to do now?

Walter,a buddy with whom I worked as an interrogation team, also a former refugee from Germany,laughed when he saw the pile of packages."I'll help you deliver them,"he offered.What else could we do?I had kept a list of the names and addresses of the people who had given me messages,so we requisitioned a closed winterized jeep and filled it with the packages.All that evening and into the night, Walter and I drove through the rubble of Vienna,dropping off parcels to surprised and grateful survivors.Most of them lived in the Soviet zone of the city.We had to drive into that area late at night,and the Soviet patrols often stopped us,suspicious.Still,we were technically allies,so we would explain that we were delivering packages to survivors of the Nazi horror and were allowed to pass unharmed.

The packages kept on coming for another week,and the mailboy grew increasingly annoyed with us.We continued our nightly deliveries all over Vienna,but I was worried that my well-intentioned offer had grown out of control.

Finally,one morning,our commanding officer called me into his office.He demanded to know why I was receiving so many parcels. Knowing that the officer was Jewish and would understand my motivation,I decided to simply tell him the truth.I admitted that I had misused the military mail to help survivors and perform a mitzvah so desperately needed.I did not expect this simple gesture to turn into this.He admonished me sternly and then smiled."We'll let it go this time,"he said,dismissing me.

Sometimes I think back to the path my little good deed had taken. Yes,it had spun out of control,but only in the way a true mitzvah does: growing and giving back again,until it has fulfilled its purpose.I was the instrument chosen to let anxious families know of the survival of loved ones.

Arnold Geier

给那些在教堂里遇见的难民的,包裹上全写着由我——阿诺德·盖尔下士转交。真是始料不及,我该怎么办?

看到成堆的包裹,与我一起在审查大队共事的好哥们沃尔特笑了,他也是一个来自德国的难民,"我来帮你一起把它们分出去。"除此之外,别无他法,好在我还留着那些托我寄信的难民的姓名和地址,我们申请借了一辆冬用吉普车,塞上成袋的包裹上路了,那一晚我和沃尔特驾车颠簸着一直忙到深夜,沿路将包裹送到那些既惊讶又心怀感激的难民手中,由于他们大多居住在这个城市的苏军占领区,我们不得不在下半夜赶到那里,满腹狐疑的苏军巡逻队还是会常常把我们拦下来,好在当时美苏两国是同盟国,我们可以解释是在给逃过纳粹魔掌的难民寄信并得以安全通行。

新的一周开始了,世界各地的包裹还是源源不断地寄来,邮递员对我们越来越恼火,我和沃尔特却还是夜复一夜的继续我们全越南的"夜间投递"活动,可我隐约有些担心,自己的好心很有可能引发不可收拾的局面。

终于,一天早上,指挥官把我请进了他的办公室,他想弄明白我为什么会收到这么多的包裹。我知道他也是犹太人,会理解我的意图的,所以决定照实说。我承认自己铤而走险滥用军用邮政帮助难民,但我没有料到事情会变成这样。指挥官狠狠训斥了我一顿,然后,他笑了,"这次我们不追究了。"说完便让我走了。

如今,我常常回想我的行善之路,对我们能力有限的人来说它的确是有些"心有余而力不足",但只有这样才是真正地做好事:善始善终直至如愿以偿。而我,则有幸被神选中,去给饱受思亲之苦的人们带来远方亲人平安的问候。

生命的彩虹

Encouraging Words
虎父无犬子

In baseball you can't let losing carry over to the next day. You've got to flip the page.

Don Baylor

棒球运动中，不能让输球的情绪持续到第二天，得想办法翻过这一页。

唐·贝勒

Someone said that encouragement is simply reminding a person of the "shoulders" he's standing on, the heritage he's been given. That's what happened when a young man, the son of a star baseball player, was drafted by one of the minor-league teams. As hard as he tried, his first season was disappointing, and by midseason he expected to be released any day.

The coaches were bewildered by his failure because he possessed all the characteristics of a superb athlete, but he couldn't seem to incorporate those advantages into a coordinated effort. He seemed to have become disconnected from his potential.

His future seemed darkest one day when he had already struck out his first time at bat. Then he stepped up to the batter's box again and quickly ran up two strikes. The catcher called a time-out and trotted to the pitcher's mound for a conference. While they were busy, the umpire, standing behind the plate, spoke casually to the boy.

Then play resumed, the next pitch was thrown—and the young man knocked it out of the park. That was the turning point. From then on,he played the game with a new confidence and power that quickly drew the attention of the parent team,and he was called up to the majors.

On the day he was leaving for the city,one of his coaches asked him what had caused such a turnaround.The young man replied that it was the encouraging remark the umpire had made that day when his baseball career had seemed doomed.

"He told me I reminded him of all the times he had stood behind my dad in the batter's box,"the boy explained."He said I was holding the bat just the way Dad had held it.And he told me, 'I can see his

有人说,所谓鼓励就是提醒他人"虎父无犬子",他们继承了祖辈优秀的禀赋和天分。故事就发生在这个棒球明星儿子的身上,年纪轻轻的他就被选拔到小职业棒球队联盟。尽管小伙子很拼命,他第一季赛事的成绩仍然令人失望,在中季比赛到来前,他随时可能走人。

所有的教练都对年轻人的成绩感到疑惑不解,他的身上具备成为一名"精英选手"的所有潜质,可他似乎无法将这些优点结合在一起完美地释放出来,他的发挥与他的潜力背道而驰。

最黑暗的一天就要到来,年轻人第一次做打击手就被三振出局,当他再次走到打击手区位时,却很快打出了两个漂亮的好球。捕手叫了暂停,快步走向投手踏板,商议对策。与此同时,站在投手板后的裁判员却和年轻人聊起天来。

比赛还在继续,又一个年轻投球手把它击出了场外,于是一切有了转机,从那以后小伙子打起比赛来总是信心满满、充满活力,很快便吸引了总队的注意,不久他就受邀加入大联盟。

临行前,一个教练问年轻人是什么让他有了"脱胎换骨"的转变,小伙子回答,就是在他的棒球事业看上去就要毁于一旦的那天,站在投球板后的裁判给了他鼓励。

"他说我的样子让他想到了那些他曾经站在我父亲身后投手区的岁月。"小伙子解释道:"裁判员告诉我,我拿球棒的样子和我父亲一模一样,

genes in you;you have your father's arms.'After that,whenever I swung the bat,I just imagined I was using Dad's arms instead of my own."

Barbara Johnson

他还说,在我身上能看到我父亲的基因,我有和我父亲一样的胳膊。从那时起,每当我挥动球棒的时候,我都会想,我是在用父亲的胳膊打球。"

Working Christmas Day
圣诞工作日

If a man loves the labor of his trade,apart from any questions of success or fame,the gods have called him.

Robert Louis Stevenson

上苍让那些爱功名的人专事耕耘他们钟情的事业。

罗伯特·路易斯·史蒂文森

It was an unusually quiet day in the emergency room on December twenty-fifth.Quiet,that is,except for the nurses who were standing around the nurses' station grumbling about having to work Christmas Day.

I was triage nurse that day and had just been out to the waiting room to clean up.Since there were no patients waiting to be seen at the time,I came back to the nurses' station for a cup of hot cider from the crockpot someone had brought in for Christmas.Just then an admitting clerk came back and told me I had five patients waiting to be evaluated.

12月25日那天,紧急救护室里异常安静,安静得只能听见几个护士围在护士台那儿轻声抱怨着圣诞节还要工作。

我是当天的分诊护士,刚刚去打扫了候诊室。因为没有病人等候就诊,我于是回到护士台,从瓦罐壶里倒了些热苹果汁,那是有人专门带来为圣诞节准备的。正在这时候,一个入院登记员跑回来告诉我已经有5个病人在等候就诊了。我抱怨道:"5个!怎么会有5个呢?我刚刚从候诊室出来的时候还一个人都没有呢!"

生命的彩虹

I whined,"Five,how did I get five?I was just out there and no one was in the waiting room."

"Well,there are five signed in."So I went straight out and called the first name.Five bodies showed up at my triage desk,a pale petite woman and four small children in somewhat rumpled clothing.

"Are you all sick?"I asked suspiciously.

"Yes,"she said weakly and lowered her head.

"Okay,"I replied,unconvinced, "who's first?"One by one they sat down,and I asked the usual preliminary questions.When it came to descriptions of their presenting problems,things got a little vague.Two of the children had headaches,but the headaches weren't accompanied by the normal body language of holding the head or trying to keep it still or squinting or grimacing.Two children had earaches,but only one could tell me which ear was affected.The mother complained of a cough but seemed to work to produce it.

Something was wrong with the picture.Our hospital policy,however,was not to turn away any patient,so we would see them.When I explained to the mother that it might be a little while before a doctor saw her because,even though the waiting room was empty,ambulances had brought in several,more critical patients,in the back,she responded, "Take your time;it's warm in here."She turned and,with a smile,guided her brood into the waiting room.

On a hunch (call it nursing judgment),I checked the chart after the admitting clerk had finished registering the family.No address—they were homeless.The waiting room was warm.

I looked out at the family huddled by the Christmas tree.The littlest one was pointing at the television and exclaiming something to her mother.The oldest one was looking at her reflection in an ornament on the Christmas tree.

I went back to the nurses' station and mentioned we had a

homeless family in the waiting room—a mother and four children between four and ten years of age.The nurses,grumbling about working
Christmas,turned to compassion for a family just trying to get warm
on Christmas.The team went into action,much as we do when there's

不过,的确有5个人登记了。于是我径直走出去喊了第一个人的名字。
接着,5个身影出现在我的办公桌前——一个脸色苍白的娇小女人和4个
小孩,身上穿的衣服看上去皱巴巴的。

"你们都生病了吗?"我问道,心里不禁猜疑。

"是的。"她轻轻应了一声就低下了头。

"好吧。"我回答,可心里还是有点怀疑。"那么谁先来呢?"待他们挨
个坐下来之后,我照例问了一些预诊的问题。但是当他们描述病状时,我
就觉得有点茫然了。其中两个孩子头痛,但是他们却没有表现出一般头痛
患者的肢体反应,比如,用手抱头、让头保持不动、眯眼、神情痛苦,等等。
另外两个孩子耳朵痛,但是只有其中一个孩子能说出来哪只耳朵被感染
了。那位母亲说是咳嗽,但那咳嗽看着像是装出来的。

这状况似乎有些不对,然而我们医院的规定是不能拒绝任何病人,所
以我们必须接收他们。我向那位妈妈解释了一番,可能要等一会儿才能见
到医生,因为尽管候诊室里没有别的病人,但是救护车已经送来几个甚至
病情更为严重的病人。她回答道:"没关系,您先忙吧。这里很暖和。"接着
她转过身,微笑着把孩子们领进了候诊室。

凭着一个护士的直觉,我觉得事情不大对劲,于是在登记员登记完那
一家5口之后,我检查了登记表。没有留地址——他们无家可归。而正如孩
子们的母亲所言"候诊室里很暖和"。

我望见他们围挤在圣诞树旁。最小的那个正指着电视机,兴致勃勃地
向她妈妈说些什么。最大的那个在看圣诞树上的装饰品里反射出来的影像。

我回到护士站,告诉大家这个特殊的情况:候诊室里无家可归的一家
人——一个妈妈带着4个4~10岁的小孩。护士们刚才还在抱怨圣诞节还要
上班,现在却可怜起这个在圣诞节只是要取点暖的一家子了。于是大家迅
速行动起来,就像在做医疗急救一样,不过这次是"圣诞急救"。

a medical emergency.But this one was a Christmas emergency.

We were all offered a free meal in the hospital cafeteria on Christmas Day,so we claimed that meal and prepared a banquet for our Christmas guests.

We needed presents.We put together oranges and apples in a basket one of our vendors had brought the department for Christmas. We made little goodie bags of stickers we borrowed from the X-ray department,candy that one of the doctors had brought the nurses, crayons the hospital had from a recent coloring contest,nurse bear buttons the hospital had given the nurses at annual training day and little fuzzy bears that nurses clipped onto their stethoscopes.We also found a mug,a package of powdered cocoa and a few other odds and ends.We pulled ribbon and wrapping paper and bells off the department's decorations that we had all contributed to.As seriously as we met the physical needs of the patients that came to us that day,our team worked to meet the needs,and exceed the expectations,of a family who just wanted to be warm on Christmas Day.

We took turns joining the Christmas party in the waiting room. Each nurse took his or her lunch break with the family,choosing to spend his or her"off-duty"time with these people whose laughter and delightful chatter became quite contagious.

When it was my turn,I sat with them at the little banquet table we had created in the waiting room.We talked for a while about dreams.The four children were telling me about what they wanted to be when they grow up.The six-year-old started the conversation. "I want to be a nurse and help people,"she declared.

After the four children had shared their dreams,I looked at the mom.She smiled and said,"I just want my family to be safe,warm and content—just like they are right now."

The "party" lasted most of the shift,before we were able to locate a shelter that would take the family in on Christmas Day.The mother had asked that their charts be pulled,so these patients were not seen that day in the emergency department.But they were treated.

As they walked to the door to leave,the four-year-old came running back,gave me a hug and whispered,"Thanks for being our angels

圣诞节那天我们在医院都有一顿免费的自助餐，于是我们用它来为我们的圣诞客人准备了一顿大餐。

我们还需要礼物。刚好有个店主专门为圣诞节送了一些橘子和苹果给我们科室，于是我们把它们统统放进一个篮子里，然后用从X光室借来的图文标签做成好看的小袋子。糖果是一个医生带来给护士们的，蜡笔是医院最近举办的涂色比赛留下的，小熊纽扣是医院在年度训练日里给护士们的，还有大家夹在听诊器上的绒毛小熊。我们还找到了一个带把儿的杯子，一袋可可粉和其他一些零碎的小东西。我们把丝带、包装纸和铃铛从医院科室的装饰物上取下来，那些本来也都是我们自己做的。正如我们认认真真地去照顾那天住院的所有病人，满足他们的护理需求一样，我们同样齐心合力地去满足一个家庭的需求，这个特殊的家庭在圣诞节这天想得到的只是一点温暖，而我们想给他们更多。

我们轮流去参加候诊室里的圣诞聚会。每个护士都利用自己的午餐休息时间与这一家子呆在一起,感受他们的欢声笑语。

轮到我的时候,我与他们一起坐在小餐桌旁,那是我们特地放在候诊室的。我们聊了聊梦想,4个孩子都告诉我他们长大了想做什么。那个6岁的孩子开口说道:"我将来想当一个护士来帮助人们。"

当4个孩子都分享了他们的梦想之后,我转向他们的妈妈。她微笑着回答:"我只是希望我的家人安全、温暖、满足,就像现在一样。"

在我们为这一家人在圣诞节找到容身之所之前,"聚会"就这样几乎持续了整个轮班时间。那位母亲让我们把他们的就诊表格取消,因此他们一家那天并没在急诊室就医。然而,实际上他们已经被大家"救护"了。

当他们走向门口准备离开时,那个4岁的小孩跑回来给了我一个拥抱并且悄悄说道:"谢谢你们,今天你们是我们的天使。"她返身跑向她的家

today."As she ran back to join her family,they all waved one more time before the door closed.I turned around slowly to get back to work,a little embarrassed for the tears in my eyes.There stood a group of my coworkers,one with a box of tissues,which she passed around to each nurse who worked a Christmas Day she will never forget.

Victoria Schlintz

人。他们在门关上的那一刹那再一次向我们挥手致意。我依依不舍地转身回去继续工作,因为眼里的泪水而有点不好意思。这时,我发现我的同事们站在那儿,其中一个手里拿着纸巾盒,她正把它传给其他护士。看来大家都度过了一个难忘的圣诞工作日。

Encouraging Kelly
鼓舞人心的凯丽

One mark of a great educator is the ability to lead
students out to new places where even the educator has
never been.

Thomas Groome

伟大的教育家的一个品质就是能够引领学生涉
猎他本人以前都没有领略的新境界、新领域。

托马斯·格鲁姆

It was my very first teaching job,and I was anxious to make an
excellent first impression.I had been hired to lead a vibrant group of
four-year-olds.As the parents escorted children into the room,I at-
tempted to deal with crying kids,teary-eyed moms and tense dads.Fi-
nally,I managed to seat the kids on the carpet and we were ready to
start our"morning circle time".

We were in the middle of a rousing rendition of "Old McDonald"
when the door opened and a mysterious woman entered the room.
She stood next to the door quietly observing the children and me.My
voice and smile never faltered,but quite frankly I was very nervous.

这是我的第一份教师工作,我极想留下完美的第一印象。我的职责是
带一帮活泼的4岁孩子。当父母护送孩子进入房间以后,我就试图对付这
群哭哭啼啼的孩子、眼泪汪汪的妈妈和紧张不安的爸爸。最后,我终于设
法让孩子们坐在了地毯上,接下来我们就要开始"早晨圈圈时间"了。

当我们正在热闹地演唱着"老麦克唐纳"的时候,门忽然开了,一个神
秘女人走了进来。她静静地站在门旁边,看着我和孩子们。我的声音没有

生命的彩虹

153

Who is this woman?Why is she here?What exactly is she observing? When I looked up again she was gone.

The day went relatively smoothly,but by the time the last child was picked up,I was physically and emotionally drained.I longed for a nonfat latte.some Chopin and a bubble bath.Then my director came in and asked to meet with me before I left for the day.

My heart raced.Did this have anything to do with the woman who had observed my class?Did I choose the wrong songs?Was the circle time too long?Too short?By the time I reached the office,I was an emotional wreck.I sat perched on the edge of my seat and waited for the axe to fall.My director told me the woman who had visited my room earlier was a potential parent to the school and was concerned about how her daughter would function in a regular classroom.Her little girl was born with a birth defect that required she wear leg braces from the kness down.The child was ambulatory but walked very slowly with a lopsided gait.She would need to be carried out to the yard and back to the classroom.Her blance was poor,and she had a tendency to topple over if she was jostled,even slightly.We would need to remind the other children to be careful when walking near her so they wouldn't accidentally cause her to fall.

The director asked me how I felt about her becoming a member of my group.I was speechless.Here I was wondering if I could possibly survive a school year with fifteen of the liveliest four-year-olds in North America,and now I was being asked to take on a child with special needs?I replied that I would accept the child on a trial basis.

That night I couldn't fall asleep.I tossed and turned until morning, then drove to work with my stomach in knots.We were all gathered on the carpet for our morning circle when the door opened and the woman walked in carrying her daughter.She introduced herself as Kelly's mommy and she gingerly sat her daughter down on the edge of the carpet.Most of the children knew Kelly from synagogue and greeted her with warm,affectionate hugs.I looked at Kelly and she looked at me."Welcome to our room,Kelly.We are so excited that you will be a member of our group."

颤抖,微笑也还挂在脸上。但是老实说,我真的紧张透顶。那个女人是谁? 她为什么来这儿?她到底在看什么?当我再次抬头看的时候,她已经走了。

那天过得还算比较顺利,但是当最后一个孩子被接走的那一刻,我突然觉得自己精疲力竭。我真想立刻来杯脱脂咖啡,一点肖邦的音乐,外加一次泡泡浴。这时候,校长走了进来,让我离开之前去一趟她的办公室。

我的心忐忑不安起来。这和来我们班观察的那个女人有关吗?我是不是选错歌了? 是不是活动时间太长? 或者太短? 当我走到办公室的时候,已经是垂头丧气了。我挨着椅子边缘坐下来,等待最后的宣判。校长告诉我,有一位家长在考虑是否要选择我们学校,就是那个早先来我班里参观的女人,她想知道她的女儿能否在一个正常的班级里活动。她的孩子出生时就是有缺陷的, 腿部膝盖以下的部分都要用支架支撑。那孩子可以行走,但只能向一边倾斜着慢慢走。她进出教室的时候必须要有人抱。她的平衡感很差,如果拥挤的话,哪怕只是轻轻挤一下,她就有可能摔倒。我们需要提醒其他的孩子,靠近她的时候一定要当心,这样他们就不会无意之中撞倒她了。

校长问我是否愿意让她成为我们班的一员。我不知该如何回答。原本我就在犹豫,自己能否在一学年里胜任、愉快地带好这15个来自北美的最活泼的孩子,而现在居然要我再带上一个需要特殊照顾的孩子。我只能回答先试试看吧。

那个晚上我失眠了,辗转反侧一直到天亮,然后揣着一颗忐忑的心开车去上班。当我们正一起在地毯上进行早晨的准备活动时,那个女人带着她的女儿走了进来。她自我介绍说是凯丽的妈妈,然后很小心地让她女儿坐在地毯的边上。大部分的孩子都知道凯丽来自犹太教会,于是用热切而真挚的拥抱来欢迎她。我和凯丽对望着,我说:"欢迎来到这儿,凯丽。我们非常高兴你将成为我们的小集体中的一员。"

The first day went really well;Kelly only fell over twice.After several days of carrying her to and form the yard,I thought,Why not encourage her to walk down the hallway a little by herself? I asked Kelly if she would like to try it,and she became very excited. The next day I sent the class out to the yard with my two assistants,and Kelly began her first journey down the hallway.She walked all the way to the next classroom,a total of ten feet.We were both thrilled! But my assistants were aghast that I was encouraging this poor child to walk.They pleaded with me to carry her outside and seat her on the bench so she could watch the other children run and play. "It would be so much easier,"they murmured.But Kelly was persistent and eager to give it her best shot.

And so we began the strenuous task of walking daily down the hall.I winced when Kelly teetered precariously too far to the right,but she just giggled and told me not to worry,she was perfectly fine.I began to cherish our quiet moments alone in the hallway,my arms outstretched to help her regain her balance. Kelly always grinned and told me she had never felt better.

Each day Kelly and I continued our slow walk down the corridor.I charted her progress with little pencil marks on the wall.Every few days the pencil marks got farther and farther apart. Kelly's class mates started to notice and began cheering for her as she plodded along.After several weeks,Kelly made it all the way to the yard! She positively glowed as the children congratulated her with gentle pats on the back and warm hugs.My assistants were astonished and prepared a special snack in honor of Kelly's tremendous accomplishment.

Weeks passed and Kelly continued to walk out to the yard every single day.We rarely carried her as she became more independent.

One week in mid-December,Kelly was absent for several days.

When I called her home I was told she was in Manhattan getting her annual checkup with her doctors.On Monday morning,When her mom brought her back to school,she inquired if I had been doing anything differently with Kelly.I wasn't quite sure what she meant.Then came the dreaded question:"Have you been forcing Kelly to walk?"

　　第一天还算顺利,凯丽只摔倒了两次。后来几天都是我抱她进出院子的,但是我想,为什么不鼓励她自己试试走过走廊呢？于是我问凯丽是否愿意自己尝试一下,她很兴奋。第二天,我和两个助手把孩子们领到院子里,而凯丽则迈出了通往走廊的第一步。她一直走完了通往另一间教室的路,一共10英尺。我们都激动得不得了。是我鼓励小凯丽独自行走的,但是我的助手们对于我的这一安排感觉惊恐不安。他们请求我把她领到外面,让她坐在长凳上,这样她就可以看着其他的孩子们奔跑和玩耍了。"那样就会容易多了。"他们低声说。但是凯丽很坚持,并且渴望能够做到最好。

　　于是我们每天都要在走廊上进行艰苦的训练。当凯丽摇摇晃晃地偏向右边的时候,我都不敢看了,但是她却咯咯地笑着叫我不要担心,说她好得很。我开始珍惜我们在走廊上的安静时光,我伸出手臂来帮她恢复平衡。凯丽总是笑着对我说她感觉好极了。

　　每一天凯丽和我都要在走廊上进行慢走练习。我用小铅笔在墙上记下她的进步。就这样铅笔记号一天天多了起来。凯丽的同学们注意到这些,于是当凯丽缓缓走过时他们就欢呼起来。过了几个星期,凯丽已经能走到院子里了。孩子们轻拍她的背或者热情地拥抱她以表示祝贺,这个时候的凯丽是真真切切的神采奕奕。我的助手们感到非常吃惊,他们准备了特别的小吃来庆祝凯丽的非凡成就。

　　几个星期过去了,凯丽照例每天都要走出院子。她越来越独立,所以我们基本不用再看护她了。

　　12月中旬的一周,凯丽好几天都没来。我打电话去她家才知道她去曼哈顿进行每年一次的医疗检查。周一的早晨,凯丽的妈妈送她来学校,她问我是不是让凯丽做了些特殊的事。我不是很理解她的意思。接着那个让我害怕的问题就来了:"你是不是让她自己走路了?"

生命的彩虹

I was dumbfounded.Maybe I shouldn't have encouraged Kelly to walk to the yard every day.Maybe I had caused permanent damage to her weakened legs.Maybe Kelly would need to be in a wheelchair for the rest of her life.

I very softly told Kelly's mom that I had encouraged her to walk outside to the yard by herself.I explained that she seemed to enjoy walking independently.The mother gently lifted Kelly's dress to show me that Kelly's knee braces had been replaced with ankle braces.

"Her legs have gotten more exercise in the past few months than in the past four years of her life."She looked at me with tears in her eyes. "I don't know how to thank you for everything you have done for my daughter."

I hugged her. "Having Kelly as a member of my group has been a privilege."

Seventeen years later,I still think back to the first time Kelly made it down the long hallway.Whenever I have a bad day teaching and life seems too overwhelming,I think of Kelly and her exuberant smile as she painstakingly walked down that hallways. She taught me that no obstacle in life is too big to overcome.You just need to keep working at it—one step at a time.

Seema Renee Gersten

我呆呆立在那儿,后悔极了。也许我不该鼓励凯丽每天走到院子去;也许我给她那双脆弱的腿带来了永久的伤害;也许凯丽的余生都要在轮椅上度过了。

　　我轻声告诉凯丽的妈妈,我是鼓励过凯丽自己走出去到院子里。我解释说凯丽似乎很喜欢独立行走。那位妈妈轻轻地提起凯丽的裙子,我看到凯丽原先的膝盖支架已经换成了脚踝支架。

　　"在过去的这几个月里,她的腿得到的锻炼比过去4年的还多。"她看着我说,眼里含着泪。"你为我的女儿做了这么多,我真不知道如何感谢你。"

　　我拥抱了她,"其实让凯丽成为我班上的一员就是我享受的特权。"

　　17年过去了,凯丽在那个长走廊里练习走路的情景还是会浮现在我脑海。每当我觉得教得不好或者生活中遇到不如意的时候,我就会想起凯丽和她在走廊上辛苦练习时露出的灿烂微笑。她教给我一个道理:生活中没有什么难关是过不了的。你要做的就是坚持不懈地去努力——每次向前迈一步。

The Plum Pretty Sister
可爱的李子妹妹

Justin was a climber.By one and a half,he had discovered the purple plum tree in the backyard,and its friendly branches became his favorite hangout.

At first he would climb just a few feet and make himself comfortable in the curve where the trunk met the branches.Soon he was building himself a small fort and dragging his toy tractors and trucks up to their new garage.

One day when he was two,Justin was playing in the tree as usual. I turned my back to prune the rosebush,and he disappeared.

"Justin,where are you?"I hollered.

His tiny voice called back,"Up here,Mommy,picking all the plums for you! "

I looked up in horror and disbelief.There was Justin on the roof of the house,filling his plastic bucket with the ripe juicy plums from his favorite tree.

When Justin was three,I became pregnant.My husband and I explained to him that we were going to have another baby as a playmate for him.

He was very excited,kissed my tummy and said, "Hello,baby,I'm your big brother,Justin."

From the beginning he was sure he was going to have a little sister,and every day he'd beg to know if she was ready to play yet. When I explained that the baby wasn't arriving until the end of June, he seemed confused.

One day he asked,"When is June,Mommy?"

I realized I needed a better explanation; how could a three-year-old know what "June" meant?Just then,as Justin climbed into the low branches of the plum tree,he gave me the answer I was looking for... his special tree.

"Justin,the baby is going to be born when the plums are ripe.You

贾斯丁简直就是个小猴子。在他一岁半的时候,他就发现了后院的那棵紫李子树,从此,那些可爱的树枝变成了他的安乐窝。

一开始,他爬几英尺就在树干和树枝交叉的地方休息。没多久,他就在那为自己建了一个堡垒,还把自己的玩具拖拉机和卡车拖进了他的新车库。

在他两岁那年,有一天,他像往常一样在树上玩。我转身去修剪蔷薇,再一回头,他就不见了。

"贾斯丁,你在哪?"我大声喊道。

他稚嫩的声音从远处飘过来:"我在上面呢,妈妈,在给你摘李子呢。"

我很担心地向上看,简直不敢相信自己的眼睛。贾斯丁拎着塑料桶站在屋顶上,桶里装满了熟透多汁的李子,是他刚从那棵心爱的李树上摘下来的。

贾斯丁3岁的时候,我又怀孕了。我和先生向他解释:我们即将有另一个小孩了,将来可以陪他一起玩。

他非常激动,亲着我的肚子说:"你好啊,小宝宝,我是你的大哥哥,贾斯丁。"

他从一开始就坚信自己将会有个小妹妹,并且每天他都要来缠着我问:她是不是可以和他一起玩了。当我向他解释小宝宝要到六月底才能来到这个世上时,他很不理解。

有一天他问我:"什么时候才到6月呀,妈妈?"

我意识到我需要给他更好的解释;一个3岁的小孩怎么能知道"6月"的意思呢?正在那时候,贾斯丁爬上那棵李子树低垂的树枝,答案霎时浮现在我的脑海中了,是那棵李子树给了我启发。

"贾斯丁,李子熟了,小宝宝就出生了,所以到时候你要通知我一声,

can keep me posted when that will be,okay?"I wasn't completely sure if I was on target,but the gardener in me was confident I'd be close enough.

Oh,he was excited!Now Justin had a way to know when his new baby sister would come to play.From that moment on,he checked the old plum tree several times a day and reported his findings to me.Of course,he was quite concerned in November when all the leaves fell off the tree.By January,with the cold and the rains,he was truly worried whether his baby would be cold and wet like his tree.He whispered to my tummy that the tree was strong and that she (the baby) had to be strong too,and make it through the winter.

By February a few purple leaves began to shoot forth,and his excitement couldn't be contained.

"My tree is growing,Mommy! Pretty soon she'll have baby plums, and then I'll have my baby sister."

March brought the plum's beautiful tiny white flowers,and Justin was overjoyed.

"She's booming,Mommy! "he chattered,struggling with the word "blooming."He rushed to kiss my tummy and got kicked in the mouth.

"The baby's moving,Mommy,she's booming,too.I think she wants to come out and see the flowers."

So it went for the next couple of months,as Justin checked every detail of his precious plum tree and reported to me about the flowers turning to tiny beads that would become plums.

The rebirth of his tree gave me ample opportunity to explain the development of the fetus that was growing inside me.Sometimes I think he believed I had actually planted a "baby seed" inside my tummy, because when I drank water he'd say things like,"You're watering our little flower,Mommy! "I'd laugh and once again explain in simple terms the story of the birds and the bees,the plants and the trees.

June finally arrived,and so did the purple plums.At first they were fairly small,but Justin climbed his tree anyway to pick some plums off the branches where the sun shone warmest.He brought

好吗？"我还拿不准这样说能否让他明白透，但是骨子里的那点园丁意识让我有了底气，觉得他理解得八九不离十了。

噢，他是多么的兴奋！现在，贾斯丁有办法知道他的小妹妹什么时候能够降临世间陪他玩耍了。从那一刻起，他每天都去查看几次那棵老李树，然后向我汇报他的新发现。当然，11月份，当那棵树的叶子都掉光的时候，他非常在意；到了1月份，天气变冷了，经常下雨，他又非常担心，担心他的小妹妹是否也像那棵树一样又湿又冷。他低声对我的肚子说：树很坚强，所以小宝宝也要一样坚强，整个冬天都要这样。

2月份的时候，树上一些紫色的新叶开始抽芽了，他简直抑制不住自己的高兴劲儿。

"我的树在长呢，妈妈！很快她就要有李子宝宝了，那么我也可以有我的小妹妹了。"

3月份，李子树上开了漂亮的小白花，可把贾斯丁乐坏了。

"她在开花呢，妈妈！"他不停地嚷，费力地要说好"开花"这两个字。他冲过来亲我的肚子，小嘴被肚子里的宝宝轻踢了一下。

"小宝宝在动，妈妈，她也在开花呢。我想她一定是想出来看花。"

接下来几个月的时间里，贾斯丁仔细盯着他心爱的李子树看，不放过每一个细枝末节，并且向我汇报说，那些花变成象小珠子一样的果子，很快就会结成李子了。

树的新生让我有了足够的时机来给贾斯丁解释体内胎儿的发育情况。有时候我觉得，他以为我是在肚子里撒下了一颗"宝宝种子"，因为我一喝水他就会说："你在给我们的小花浇水呢，妈妈。"我总是笑着，又一次用简单的语言跟他说明，小宝宝是怎样来到妈妈肚子里的。

6月份终于到了，紫李子也熟了。一开始李子都很小，但是贾斯丁还是要爬到树上，从日照较多的树枝上摘下一些李子。他把它们拿给我看，让

them to me to let me know the baby wasn't ripe yet.

I felt ripe! I was ready to pop! When were the plums going to start falling from that darn tree?

Justin would rub my tummy and talk to his baby sister,telling her she had to wait a little longer because the fruit was not ready to be picked yet.His forays into the plum tree lasted longer each day,as if he was coaxing the tree to ripen quickly.He talked to the tree and thanked it for letting him know about this important event in his life. Then one day,it happened.Justin came running into the house,his eyes as big as saucers,with a plastic bucket full to the brim of juicy purple plums.

"Hurry,Mommy,hurry! "he shouted. "She's coming,she's coming! The plums are ripe,the plums are ripe! "

I laughed uncontrollably as Justin stared at my stomach,as if he expected to see his baby sister erupt any moment.That morning I did feel a bit queasy,and it wasn't because I had a dental appointment. Before we left the house,Justin went out to hug his plum tree and whisper that today was the day his "plum pretty sister" would arrive. He was certain.

As I sat in the dental chair,the labor pains began,just as Justin had predicted.Our "plum" baby was coming! I called my parents,and my husband rushed me to the hospital.At 6:03 p.m.on June 22,the day that will forever live in family fame as "Plum Pretty Sister Day,"our daughter was born.We didn't name her Purple Plum as Justin suggested,but chose another favorite flower,Heather.

At Heather's homecoming,Justin kissed his new playmate and presented her with his plastic bucket,full to the brim with sweet,ripe, purple plums.

"These are for you,"he said proudly.

Justin and Heather are now teenagers,and the plum tree has become our bonding symbol.Although we moved from the home that housed Justin's favorite plum tree,the first tree to be planted in our new yard was a purple plum,so that Justin and Heather could know when to expect her special day.Throughout their growing-up years,the

我知道小宝宝还没成熟呢。

可是我感觉已经到时间了,我觉得自己快要炸开了。究竟什么时候那些李子才会从那要命的树上掉下来啊?

贾斯丁摸着我的肚子跟他的小妹妹说话,告诉她还得再等一段时间,因为还没到采摘果实的时候。每天他和树纠缠的时间又长了些,似乎是在哄着树成熟得快点。他和树谈心,感谢树让他知道了自己生命中这件重要的事。后来有一天,他终于如愿以偿了。贾斯丁连蹦带跳地跑进屋子,眼睛瞪得茶托一样大,手里的塑料桶里装满了多汁的紫李子。

"快点,妈妈,快点啊!"他叫着。"她来了,她来了!李子熟了,李子熟了!"

当贾斯丁盯着我的肚子看的时候,我止不住地笑,他好像在期待着小妹妹随时蹦出来。那天早晨我确实觉得有些不适,这不适感并非因为我约了牙医而导致的。在我们离开之前,贾斯丁跑出去拥抱了李子树,并且轻声说,今天他那"可爱的李子妹妹"就会降临,他肯定。

当我坐在牙科椅子上,阵痛开始了,就像贾斯丁预测的一样。我们的"李子"宝宝要出来了!我打电话给我父母,我先生急匆匆地把我送进医院。在6月22日下午6点3分,我们的女儿出生了,那天被命名为"可爱李子妹妹日",并且永远被我们铭记在心。我们没有按照贾斯丁的建议叫她紫李子,而是用了另外一种我们喜欢的花的名字:石楠。

当石楠回家的时候,贾斯丁吻着她,并且把他的塑料桶作为礼物送给她,桶里是满满的、甜甜的、熟透的紫李子。

"这些是给你的。"他很自豪地说。

贾斯丁和石楠现在已经是十几岁的少年了,而李子树也成为我们一家人的信物。尽管我们后来搬家了,离开了那个给贾斯丁最爱的李子树提供荫庇的地方,但是我们在新院子里种的第一棵树就是紫李子树,这样贾

children spent countless hours nestled in the branches,counting down the days through the birth of leaves,flowers,buds and fruit.Our birthday parties are always festooned with plum branches and baskets brimming with freshly picked purple plums.Because as Mother Nature—and Justin—would have it,for the last fifteen years, the purple plum has ripened exactly on June 22.

Cynthia Brian

斯丁和石楠就知道什么时候是那个特殊的日子了。在孩子们成长的那些年,他们经常依偎在树枝下,通过树叶的发芽、开花、结果来计算日月。我们的生日聚会也总是用李子树枝和装满新鲜李子的篮子做装饰。因为在过去的15年里,或许是由于成熟周期,又或许是贾斯丁使然,那棵李子树的紫色果实总是很守时地在6月22那天成熟。

Turkeys
纯种火鸡

Something about my mother attracts ornithologists.It all started years ago when a couple of them discovered she had a rare species of woodpecker coming to her bird feeder.They came in the house and sat around the window,exclaiming and taking pictures with big fancy cameras.But long after the red cockaded woodpeckers had gone to roost,the ornithologists were still there.There always seemed to be three or four of them wandering around our place and staying for supper.

In those days,during the 1950s,the big concern of ornithologists in our area was the wild turkey.They were rare,and the pure-strain wild turkeys had begun to interbreed with farmers' domestic stock. The species was being degraded.It was extinction by dilution,and to the ornithologists it was just as tragic as the more dramatic demise of the passenger pigeon or the Carolina parakeet.

有件关于我母亲的事，引起了鸟类学家的注意。这一切发生在多年前，有两个鸟类学家发现有只稀有品种的啄木鸟在吃母亲喂食器里的食物。他们进了屋，坐在窗旁，高兴地叫着，用昂贵的相机照相。可在红冠啄木鸟离去歇着很久之后，鸟类学家还待着不走。他们似乎总有三四个人在我们家转悠，而且留下来吃晚饭。

在20世纪50年代，我们这一地区鸟类学家最关心的是稀有的野火鸡。纯种野火鸡已经和农户的家养火鸡混种，品种质量有所下降。混种将导致野火鸡灭绝，对鸟类学家来说，这和北美候鸽或卡罗来纳长尾小鹦鹉大批大批地死亡同样悲惨。

有个鸟类学家设计了一种计算公式，对家养火鸡和纯种火鸡进行起

生命的彩虹

167

One ornithologist had devised a formula to compute the ratio of domestic to pure-strain wild turkey in an individual bird by comparing the angle of flight at takeoff and the rate of acceleration.And in those sad days,the turkeys were flying low and slow.

It was during that time,the spring when I was six years old,that I caught the measles.I had a high fever,and my mother was worried about me.She kept the house quiet and dark and crept around silently,trying different methods of cooling me down.

Even the ornithologists stayed away—but not out of fear of the measles or respect for a household with sickness.The fact was,they had discovered a wild turkey nest.According to the formula,the hen was pure-strain wild—not a taint of the sluggish domestic bird in her blood—and the ornithologists were camping in the woods,protecting her nest from predators and taking pictures.

One night our phone rang.It was one of the ornithologists. "Does your little girl still have measles?"he asked.

"Yes,"said my mother."She's very sick.Her temperature is 102."

"I'll be right over,"said the ornithologist.

In five minutes a whole carload of them arrived.They marched solemnly into the house,carrying a cardboard box. "A hundred and two,did you say?Where is she?"they asked my mother.

They crept into my room and set the box down on the bed.I was barely conscious,and when I opened my eyes,their worried faces hovering over me seemed to float out of the darkness like giant, glowing eggs.They snatched the covers off me and felt me all over. They consulted in whispers.

"Feels just right,I'd say."

"A hundred two—can't miss if we tuck them up close and she lies still."

I closed my eyes then,and after a while the ornithologists drifted

away,their pale faces bobbing up and down on the black wave of
fever.

The next morning I was better.For the first time in days I could
think.The memory of the ornithologists with their whispered voices

飞角度和加速度的比较。在那些令鸟类学家关切的岁月里,火鸡飞得又低
又慢。

就在那个时期,在我6岁那年的春天,我得了麻疹,发着高烧,我妈妈
十分担心。她把家里保持得很安静,屋中暗暗的,走路轻轻地,想方设法让
我平静。

甚至那些鸟类学家也都离开了, 但不是因为怕传染上麻疹或家有病
人出于礼貌。事实是,他们发现了一个野火鸡窝。根据公式计算,那雌火鸡
是纯种,没有沾上一丝家养火鸡品种的不良成分。为了拍照和保护那个窝
不受捕食动物的侵扰,鸟类学家们在树林里扎营露宿。

有天晚上,电话铃响了,是一个鸟类学家打来的。他问道,"你那小女
孩麻疹还没好吗?"

"对,没好,"我妈妈回答说,"病得挺厉害,发烧102度(华氏)。"

"我马上过来,"对方说。

5分钟之后,来了一车人。他们大步走了进来,面目严肃,拿着一个纸
板箱。"你是说102度吗? 她在哪儿?"他们问我母亲。

他们蹑手蹑脚地走进我的房间,把箱子放在我床上。我昏昏沉沉,似
醒非醒;等我睁开眼睛一看,他们那忧心忡忡的脸色就像从黑暗中浮现的
发光的巨型蛋停在我头上。他们掀开被子,摸摸我全身,然后窃窃私语商
量着什么。

"我觉得正合适。"

"102度——要是把它们塞得靠近点儿,她不动的话,能行。"

我当时闭着眼。过了片刻,那些鸟类学家逐渐离去。我发着烧,在昏睡
中就觉得他们那苍白的脸在黑色浪涛里上下摆动。

第二天早上我感觉好些,多少天来第一次感到神志清醒了。记忆中鸟
类学家和他们的轻声低语像是生活在另一个世界的一场梦。但当我拉开

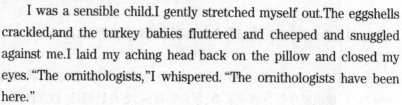

was like a dream from another life.But when I pulled down the covers, there staring up at me with googly eyes and wide mouths were sixteen fuzzy baby turkeys,and the cracked chips and caps of sixteen brown speckled eggs.

I was a sensible child.I gently stretched myself out.The eggshells crackled,and the turkey babies fluttered and cheeped and snuggled against me.I laid my aching head back on the pillow and closed my eyes. "The ornithologists,"I whispered. "The ornithologists have been here."

It seems the turkey hen had been so disturbed by the elaborate protective measures that had been undertaken on her behalf that she had abandoned her nest on the night the eggs were due to hatch.It was a cold night.The ornithologists,not having an incubator on hand, used their heads and came up with the next best thing.

The baby turkeys and I gained our strength together.When I was finally able to get out of bed and feebly creep around the house,the turkeys peeped and cheeped around my ankles,scrambling to keep up with me and tripping over their own big spraddle-toed feet.When I went outside for the first time,the turkeys tumbled after me down the steps and scratched around in the yard while I sat in the sun.

Finally,in late summer,the day came when they were ready to fly for the first time as adult birds.The ornithologists gathered.I ran down the hill,and the turkeys ran too.Then,one by one,they took off. They flew high and fast.The ornithologists made Vs with their thumbs and forefingers,measuring angles.They consulted their stop-watches and paced off distances.They scribbled in their tiny notebooks.Finally they looked at each other.They sighed.They smiled.They jumped up and down and hugged each other. "One hundred percent pure wild turkey! "they said.

Nearly forty years have passed since then.Now there's a vaccine for measles.And the woods where I live are full of pure wild turkeys.I like to think they are all descendants of those sixteen birds I saved from the vigilance of the ornithologists.

被子,便看到16只毛茸茸的雏火鸡张大嘴睁大眼睛瞪着我,还有16个棕色带斑纹的破蛋壳和一些碎壳片。

　　我是个懂事的孩子。我慢慢地挪开身子。蛋壳裂开了,初生的火鸡拍动着翅膀,唧唧地叫着,偎依着我。我又把阵阵疼痛的头靠在枕头上,闭上了眼。"研究鸟的人,"我低声说道,"那些鸟类学家来过了。"

　　看来采取的悉心保护措施惊扰了那只雌火鸡,该孵蛋的那天晚上它弃窝而去。天气很冷,那些鸟类学家手头又没有孵化器,灵机一动就想到了这样的最佳方案。

　　我恢复体力的同时,雏火鸡也逐渐成长。我终于能下地了,有气无力地在屋里地上爬,它们在我两膝旁唧唧叫着,竞相跟上我,还不时绊倒在自己的大叉趾脚上。病愈头一次出屋时,火鸡们跟着我跌跌撞撞下了台阶。我坐着晒太阳,它们在院子里到处扒土。

　　夏天即将过去,已经长成成鸟的火鸡初次飞翔的日子来临了,鸟类学家们又聚集一起。我跑下小山,火鸡也跟着跑。然后,一个接着一个离地飞得又高又快。鸟类学家们用大拇指和食指构成V形量测角度。他们查看秒表,步测距离,在小笔记本上写下什么。最后他们互相看看,宽慰地舒了口气,脸上绽出了微笑,然后欢呼雀跃,相互拥抱。他们说:"百分之百的纯种野火鸡!"

　　打那以后将近40年过去了,如今已经有麻疹疫苗。我所住的林子里满是纯种野火鸡。一想到它们都是在鸟类学家警觉下由我拯救的那16只火鸡的后代,我就感到高兴。

Stressbusters
压力杀手

> *Therefore do not be anxious about tomorrow, for tomorrow will be anxious for itself.Let the day's own trouble be sufficient for the day.*
>
> Matthew 6:34

"千万不要为明天忧虑,因为明天自有明天的忧虑,一天的难处一天担当就够了。"

马太福音

As a college freshman at Valparaiso University,facing all the uncertainties of future academic and work life,I had the opportunity to meet with the president emeritus and chancellor.Audiences were rare.Sitting among a small group of nervous peers,we anxiously awaited the arrival of a man revered throughout the school,let alone the country and abroad,for his excellence in achievement and esteemed wisdom.

Dr. O. P. Kretzman arrived in a wheelchair,aging,with failing sight. You could have heard a pin drop.All too soon,the attention turned to us as he asked for questions from the group.Silence.I knew inside what an opportunity this was,so despite my fear,I got up the courage to break the ice and ask my question.

"What advice would you give new freshman as we face all the choices and uncertainties ahead of us?"His reply was simple and strong, "Take one bite out of the apple at a time."No more,no less.A perfect stressbuster for the moment and for all the moments of my life to come.

Now that I've been in the working world for 20 years,I've added a few more stressbusters to maintain a healthy life.Help yourself!

1.Change your priorities

2.Take stretch breaks

3.Step back and observe

4.Review your purpose

5.Get a massage

6.Leave five minutes earlier

7.See a comedy

8.Let go and let God!

9.Use affirmations

10.Organize your space

11.Share your feelings

12.Smell some flowers

当我还在瓦尔帕莱索(智利中部一港口城市)大学上大一的时候,面对未来漫长的学业与工作,我感到一片茫然。当时我有一个机会,得以见到我们学校的荣誉校长。那天在场的听众很少,只有我们这一届的一些学生,我和众人一起,坐在那里焦急地等待这位大人物的出现。他不但在校内,而且在全国甚至国外也备受尊敬,他在学术上卓越的成就与惊人的智慧令人景仰。

克瑞兹曼博士坐着轮椅进场,显得苍老不堪,两眼无目的地四处观望,室内静得连一根针掉下都听得见。很快地,他把注意力转到我们身上,因为他要我们提出问题。这时一片寂静,我心里明白,这是个多么难得的机会,于是勉强按捺心中的恐惧,鼓起勇气,打破室内的沉默,提出我的疑问。

"对于这样一群青年人,他们面对将来各种选择和变化莫测的世事,你会给些什么样的建议呢?"他的回答简单有力:"一次只咬一口苹果。"就这样,不多不少,对当时的我以及我后来的一生而言,这句话就是再好也不过的压力杀手。

如今我已经踏入社会20年,我自己对这个压力杀手也添加了一些我的看法,以维持健康的生活。现整理如下:

1.改变优先顺序

2.延长休息时间

3.退一步观察一下环境

4.重新检视自己的目标

5.找人帮自己按摩一下

6.提早五分钟离开

7.欣赏一部喜剧

8.放手把一切交给上帝!

9.运用肯定的说法

10.充分利用空间,一切保持井井有条

11.和别人分享自己的感受

12.闻闻花香

13.Ask for acknowledgment

14.Listen to your intuition

15.Help someone else

16.Rub your feet and hands

17.Visualize positive outcomes

18.Take care of your health

19.Don't judge;bless

20.Work in the garden

21.Create a budget

22.Be empathetic,not overly sensitive

23.Be still and meditate

24.Use time-saving technology

25.Carpool and enjoy the ride

26.Set aside time for planning

27.Count your blessings

28.Don't forget,write it down

29.Simplify,simplify,simplify

30.Talk it out with coworkers

31.Eliminate destructive self-talk

32.Schedule play time

33.Change your environment

34.Go with your natural rhythms

35.Find an easy place to give your gifts

36.Fully express yourself

37.View problems as opportunities

38.Let go of"what ifs"

39.Be clear what's expected of you

40.Ask the experts

41.Do your best and then stop

42.Trust Divine timing and order

43.Develop patience

44.Breathe deeply

45.Take a walk

46.Complete things

47.Take a nap

48.Sing a tune

49.Take a warm bath

50.Talk out your worries

51.Delegate

52.Talk with your mom or dad

53.Say no at times

54.Shift deadlines

55.Follow your passion

56.Tell a joke

57.Play out your fears

58.Drink lots of good water

59.Create a support system

60.Divide up big projects

61.Seek advice

62.Be gentle with yourself

63.Don't"enable"others

64.Pray for openings

65.Tell the truth

66.Get more restful sleep

67.Forgive and move on

68.Prepare food ahead

13.要求答谢

14.听从自己的直觉

15.帮助他人

16.摩擦双脚与双手

17.想像积极的结果

18.照顾自己的身体

19.不作判决,祝福就行了

20.享受种花栽草的乐趣

21.拟出预算

22.要设身处地思考问题,不要过度
敏感

23.保持镇定和沉思的习惯

24.运用省时的技巧

25.合伙使用汽车,享受搭车的乐趣

26.拟出制订计划的时间

27.回顾自己得到的祝福

28.别丢三落四,把待办的事情写下
来

29.简化、简化、再简化

30.和同事开诚布公地讨论,解决一
切疑难

31.避免对自己说丧气话

32.规划出一些玩耍的时间

33.改变四周的环境

34.顺应天然的韵律

35.送礼物时,找个容易出手的地方

36.完整表达自己的意见

37.视危机为转机

38.别去想"如果……就好了"

39.弄清楚自己的义务

40.请教专家

41.尽力去做,然后放手休息

42.信赖上天的时间选择和指示

43.培养耐性

44.深呼吸

45.散散步

46.把事情做完

47.睡个午觉

48.唱唱曲调

49.洗个热水澡

50.说出内心的忧虑

51.委派别人代劳

52.与父亲或母亲谈一谈

53.有时要懂得拒绝别人

54.修改完成期限

55.追随自己的激情

56.说个笑话

57.尽情宣泄内心的恐惧

58.喝下许多甜美的水

59.建构一个可以提供支援的体系

60.把大型计划分成许多部分来执行

61.听取别人的劝告

62.温柔对待自己

63.别给他人欺负你的借口

64.祈祷能获得发展事业的有利条
件

65.说实话

66.睡得更安稳、更久一些

67.原谅他人的错误,既往不咎

68.预先多准备一些食物

69.Fix it or get a new one

70.Be prepared to wait

71.Don't always be right

72.Focus on the moment

73.Take a lunch break

74.Read a book

75.Shift your attitude

76.Laugh each day

77.Develop self-esteem

78.Take vitamin supplements

79.Stop the"shoulds"

80.Avoid excess

81.Plan a special outing

82.See through illusions

83.Relax your muscles

84.Slow down and notice

85.Nurture good friends

86.Be in nature

87.Listen to music

88.Limit caffeine and sugar

89.Go on a fast or cleanse

90.Be spontaneous

91.Love your partner

92.Get some fresh air

93.Be pampered

94.Volunteer

95.Join help networks

96.Maintain good posture

97.Respect your limits

98.Exercise routinely

99.Go dancing

100.Sigh occasionally

101.Do yoga

102.Have a good cry

103.Make time for hobbies

104.Limit work time

105.Compromise/cooperate

106.Don't procrastinate

107.Unplug your phone/TV

108.Relax your standards

109.Journal your thoughts

110.Take a vacation

111.Organize your desk

112.Develop flexibility

113.Allow for imperfections

114.Don't over-schedule

115.Expose your secrets

116.Build a strong body

117.Nurture your faith

118.Open a savings account

119.Take in the sun

120.Love and be loved

121.Get the facts

122.Work as a team

123.Smile—open your heart

124.Validate yourself

125.Daydream

126.Know God loves you!

Tim Clauss

双语精华版心灵鸡汤·

69.把东西修理好,不然就买个新的

70.有等人的心理准备

71.别老是当正确的一方

72.专心处理眼前的事

73.午餐时休息一下

74.读本书

75.改变自己的态度

76.每天笑一笑

77.培养自尊

78.补充维生素

79.别再提"我应该……"

80.避免过渡

81.计划一次特别的远足

82.看穿幻象

83.放松肌肉

84.放松脚步,注意身边的事物

85.培养稳固的友谊

86.亲近大自然

87.听听音乐

88.限制糖和咖啡因的摄取

89.斋戒沐浴,清心养性

90.让感情自然流露

91.喜爱你的伙伴

92.呼吸一些新鲜空气

93.享受受宠的感觉

94.自愿做某些事

95.自愿担任义工、守望相助或帮
   助他人

96.保持良好的姿势

97.接受自己的极限

98.固定做运动

99.跳跳舞

100.偶尔叹叹气

101.做瑜伽

102.好好哭一场

103.安排时间享受自己的嗜好

104.限制工作时间

105.折中彼此的意见以助于合作

106.不要犹豫不决

107.拔去电话及电视的插头

108.降低标准

109.记下自己的想法

110.好好度个假

111.清理书桌,让物归原位

112.培养弹性

113.接受瑕疵

114.别计划做太多事

115.说出心底的秘密

116.培养强壮的身体

117.培养自己的信仰

118.开一个储蓄账户

119.晒晒太阳

120.爱别人与被人爱

121.认清事实

122.团队合作

123.多微笑——打开心扉

124.证实自己的论点

125.做做白日梦

The Deer and the Nursing Home
疗伤的鹿

CHICKEN SOUP

The deer had been struck and killed by a car.A passing motorist on the narrow mountain road saw a slight movement and stopped. Huddled beside the dead deer was a fawn with the umbilical cord still attached. "I don't suppose you have a chance,"the motorist told the tiny creature as he tied off the cord, "but at least I'll take you where it's warm."

The nearest place was the powerhouse of New Jersey's Glen Gardner Center for Geriatrics,a state institution.Maintenance men there quickly produced rags to make a bed behind the boiler for the fawn.Then they took a rubber glove,pricked pinholes in a finger,diluted some milk and offered it to the fawn,who drank eagerly.

With the men taking turns feeding the fawn,the little deer's wobbly legs and curiosity soon grew strong enough to bring it out from its bed behind the boiler.On their breaks,the men petted and played with the baby. "If it's a female,we'll call her Jane Doe,"they laughed. But it was a male,so they taught him to answer to"Frankie,"short for Frank Buck.

Frankie became especially attached to one of the men,an electrician named Jean.On nice days,Frankie stepped outside with his new friend,enjoying the fresh air and scratches behind the ears.Sometimes other deer came out of the woods to graze.When Frankie caught their scent,his head came up.

"You'd better tie him or we'll lose him,"someone commented.

Jean shook his head."He'll know when it's time to go,"he said.

Frankie began following Jean on his rounds,and the slight,white-haired man followed by the delicate golden fawn soon became a familiar sight.

One day a resident,noticing Frankie waiting by a door for Jean, invited the deer in.Glen Gardner housed old people who had been in state mental hospitals and needed special care.When Frankie was discovered inside,the staff rushed to put him outside.But when they saw

那只鹿被一辆汽车撞死了。一个在狭窄山路上经过的驾车人看见有个什么东西微微动了几下,就停了下来。蜷缩在死鹿旁的是头脐带尚未断开的初生幼鹿。"我想你活下来的机会很小,"驾车人一边给脐带打结一边对这个小生灵说,"但至少我要把你带到一个暖和的地方。"

最近的地方是新泽西州州立格伦加德纳老年医学中心的电工房,那里的工作人员立即拿出碎布,在锅炉后面给小鹿铺了张床。然后,他们找来一只橡胶手套,在一个指头上扎了几个洞眼,灌上稀释的牛奶喂小鹿。小鹿迫不及待地喝了起来。

工作人员轮流喂奶,小鹿晃晃悠悠的腿很快长得有劲起来,好奇心也随之增长,开始从锅炉后面的床出来。工作人员一休息,就摸摸它,逗它玩。他们笑着说:"它要是母的,就叫它简·多伊。"但是它是头公鹿。他们教它熟悉"费兰基"这个名字,这是雄鹿费兰克的简称。

费兰基尤其喜欢他们当中一个叫简的电工。天气好的时候,费兰基和它的新朋友一起出来,享受清新的空气并搔搔耳背。有时,别的鹿从树林里出来吃草,费兰基闻见它们的气味时,就抬起头来。

有人建议说,"最好拴上它,要不然会丢的。"

简摇头表示不同意。他说:"到该走的时候,它会知道的。"

费兰基开始尾随简巡视。不久,瘦小、白发的电工后面跟着纤弱、金黄色的小鹿就成了人们熟悉的景象。

有一天,格伦加德纳疗养中心的一位老人看见弗兰基在门旁等简,就把小鹿带了进去。疗养中心住着在州立精神病院接受过治疗、需要特别照顾的老年人。工作人员一发现小鹿,就急忙要把它轰走。但是当他们看到住在这里的人们都急不可耐地伸出手去摸它,就让小鹿留下了。从此每当

how eagerly one resident after another reached out to touch him,they let him stay.When Frankie appeared,smiles spread and people who seldom spoke asked the deer's name.

Discovering a line in front of the payroll clerk's window one day, Frankie companionably joined it.When his turn came,the clerk peered out at him. "Well,Frankie,"she said, "I wouldn't mind giving you a paycheck.You're our best social worker! "

The deer had the run of Glen Gardner until late fall,when the superintendent noticed he was growing antlers.Fearful he might accidentally injure a resident,the supervisor decreed banishment.Frankie continued to frequent the grounds,but as the months passed he explored farther afield.When he was a year old,the evening came when he didn't return to the powerhouse;now he was on his own.

Still,every morning he was there to greet Jean,exploring the pocket for the treat Jean always brought,and in the afternoon he would reappear.Residents who had refused to go outside before would join him on the front lawn to scratch his ears.George,a solitary resident with a speech defect who didn't seem to care if people understood him or not,taught Frankie to respond to his voice,and they often walked together.

When Frankie was two years old—a sleek creature with six-point antlers and a shiny coat—he failed to show up one April morning.Nor did he answer anyone's calls.It was late the next day before Jean and George found him lying on a sheltered patch of ground.His right front leg was shattered,jagged splinters of bone jutted through the skin.

"Oh,you old donkey,"Jean whispered. "What happened?"The deer's eyes were clouded with pain,but he knew Jean's voice and tried to lick his hand.

"There's no way to set a break like that without an operation," said the veterinarian who examined Frankie.They would have to haul

Frankie out of the woods on an improvised litter and drive him to Round Valley Veterinary Hospital, five miles away.

On the day of Frankie's surgery, the surgeon, Dr. Gregory Zolton, told Jean, "You'll have to stay with me while I operate. I'll need help."

弗兰基一出现，到处可见的是微笑，连那些平常极少说话的老人也打听小鹿叫什么名字。

一天，弗兰基发现发工资的窗口前面有人排着队，它也跟着人们排队。轮到它时，负责发工资的工作人员盯着它说道："是啊，弗兰基，我真想给你张支票。你是我们最好的社会工作者！"

暮秋前，弗兰基在疗养中心一直行动自由。直到有一天，中心的主管注意到它开始长角了。中心负责人担心它会意外伤着住在这里的老人，决定禁止它自由出入。弗兰基仍常去附近的场地。随着时光流逝，它去更远的田野探索。年满1岁后的一天傍晚，它没有回到老年中心的电工房，它开始独立生活了。

每天早上，弗兰基依旧来和简打招呼，把嘴伸到他口袋里找为它准备的好吃的东西。下午它再次出现。疗养中心那些原来不愿意出来的老人们也开始来到楼前草地搔它的耳朵。乔治是个有语言障碍、不合群的老人，他从不在乎别人是否理解他，但他教会弗兰基对他的语声做出反应。他们俩经常在一起散步。

弗兰基两岁时，毛色油亮，长着六叉茸角。4月的一个早晨，它没有露面。谁叫它都没有回应。第二天晚些时候，简和乔治发现它躺在有遮掩的地面上，右前腿折断，露出锯齿状的碎骨。

"哦，你这个家伙，"简喃喃地说着，"出了什么事？"弗兰基的目光因痛苦而混浊。但它听出简的声音，尽力去舔他的手。

给弗兰基做检查的兽医说："这样的骨折，不动手术是没法接骨的。"他们得把弗兰基用临时拼成的担架从树林里抬出来，开车把它送到5英里以外的兽医院去。

动手术那天，主刀的格雷戈里·佐尔顿医生对简说，"我给它开刀的时候，你得待在这儿。我需要帮助。"简听了这话，胃里一阵翻腾，但他使劲往

Jean's stomach did a flip-flop, but he swallowed hard and nodded. During the two-hour procedure, Dr. Zolton took bone from Frankie's shoulder to make a graft between the broken bones and then screwed a steel plate across it.

"He said a leg that wasn't strong enough to run on wasn't any good to a deer," recalls Jean.

After the surgery, they took Frankie to an unused horse stable on Glen Gardner's grounds, and Jean sat in the straw beside the recovering deer. He stroked Frankie's head and held him whenever the deer tried to struggle to his feet. Finally, as the sun was coming up, Jean took his own stiff bones home, cleaned up and went to work.

By the seventh day, Jean called Dr. Zolton to say it was impossible to hold Frankie still for his antibiotic injections. The surgeon laughed. "If he's that lively, he doesn't need antibiotics." But he warned that Frankie must be kept inside for eight weeks. If he ran on the leg before it knitted, it would shatter.

"Whenever anyone went to visit him, Frankie showed how eager he was to get out," recalls Jean. "He'd stand there with his nose pressed against a crack in the door. He smelled spring coming."

When word had come that Frankie had survived the operation, the residents' council at Glen Gardner had called a meeting. Mary, the president, told the group, "There's no operation without a big bill. Now, Frankie's our deer, right?" The residents all nodded. "So we've got to pay his bill." They decided to take up a collection and hold a bake sale.

The day Dr. Zolton's bill arrived, Mary called a meeting. The others watched silently as she opened the envelope. "Oh, dear," she murmured bleakly, "we owe $392." They had managed to collect only $135. Not until she shifted her bifocals did she notice the handwriting, which read: "Paid in Full—Gregory Zolton, D.V.M."

When Frankie's confinement was over,Frankie's friends gathered by the stable door.It was mid-June and grass was knee-deep in the meadow.The buck's wound was beautifully healed—but would the leg hold?

Jean opened the barn door. "Come on,Frankie,"he said softly. "You can go now."Frankie took a step and looked up at Jean.

下咽,点头表示同意。佐尔顿医生从弗兰基的肩膀取骨移接在断骨之间,然后用一块钢板固定,用了两个小时。

事后简回忆说:"医生当时说,鹿要是靠一条吃不住劲的腿跑的话可不行。"

手术之后,他们把弗兰基带到疗养中心场地上的一处弃置不用的马厩里,简坐在麦秆上,陪着恢复中的鹿。每当它想站起来,他就摸摸它的头把它按下去。待到天亮,简才拖着僵硬的身子回家,洗漱后去上班。

到了第7天,简打电话告诉佐尔顿医生说,给弗兰基打抗生素时没法按住它。医生听了就笑,说:"如果它有那么大的劲,就不需要抗生素了。"但是,他警告说弗兰基必须在户内呆8个星期,如果骨头没愈合,出去跑会断的。

"每当有人来看弗兰基时,它总是表现得急于外出,"简回忆说,"它站在那儿把鼻子贴在门缝上。它闻到了春天的气息。"

弗兰基手术成功的消息传来后,疗养中心病人理事会召开了会议。主席玛丽告诉与会者说:"手术费总是很贵的。弗兰基是咱们的鹿,对吧?"大家都点头同意。"所以得由我们支付这笔费用。"他们决定举办一次烘烤食品义卖进行募捐。

佐尔顿医生账单来的那天,玛丽又召开了一次会。在她撕开信封的时候,大家都屏气瞧着她。"我的天啊!"她忧郁地低声说道,"我们得付392块钱。"但是他们只募集到135块钱。直到她推动双焦点眼镜的时候才注意到一行字:已全额付清——兽医学博士格雷戈里·佐尔顿。

弗兰基幽禁期结束时,它的朋友们聚集在马厩门旁。那时是6月中旬,草已经长到人的膝盖一般高。雄鹿的伤口愈合得非常好,但是它的腿能支

"It's all right,"Jean urged him. "You're free."Suddenly Frankie understood.He exploded into a run,flying over the field like a greyhound,his hooves barely touching the ground.

"He's so glad to be out,"Mary said wistfully, "I don't think we'll ever see him again."

At the edge of the woods,Frankie swerved.He was coming back! Near the stable he wheeled again.Six times he crossed the meadow. Then,flanks heaving,tongue lolling,he pulled up beside them.Frankie had tested his leg to its limits.It was perfect. "Good! "said George distinctly.Everyone cheered.

Soon Frankie was again waiting for Jean by the electric shop every morning.In the fall Jean put a yellow collar around Frankie's neck to warn off hunters.The mountain was a nature preserve,with no hunting allowed,but poachers frequently sneaked in.

One day a pickup truck filled with hunters drove up to the powerhouse.When the tailgate was lowered,Frankie jumped down.The hunters had read about him and,spotting the yellow collar,figured it must be Frankie.

Every hunting season,George and the other people at Glen Gardner debate whether to lock Frankie in the stable for his own safety— and their peace of mind.But each fall,the vote always goes against it. Frankie symbolizes the philosophy of Glen Gardner,which is to provide care but not to undermine independence.

"A deer and a person,they each have their dignity,"Jean says. "You mustn't take their choices away."

So Frank Buck,the wonderful deer of Glen Gardner,remains free. He runs risks,of course,but life is risk,and Frankie knows he has friends he can count on.

Jo Coudert

撑它的身体吗?

简把马厩门打开。"出来吧,弗兰基,"他轻声细语地说道,"你可以走了。"

那鹿向前迈了一步,抬头瞧着简。"没事了,"简鼓励它,"你自由了。"弗兰基骤然明白了。它猛地奔跑起来,像一头灰狗一样飞越跑过旷野,四蹄几乎腾空。

"它非常高兴能出来了,"玛丽若有所思地说,"我想我们再也见不到它了。"

在树林边上,弗兰基突然转过身来。它回来了!到了马厩,又回头再飞跑,连续6次横穿草地。然后,喘着气,伸着舌头,慢慢地走进人群。弗兰基测试了伤腿的最大承受能力,证明它完全正常。"好!"乔治语气肯定地说道。在场的人无不喝彩欢呼。

不久,每天早上弗兰基又在电工房等着简。秋天时,简给弗兰基套上个黄脖圈,告诫猎人不要猎杀它。那个山区是个自然保护区,不准狩猎,但总有些非法盗猎者偷偷潜入。

一天,一辆小货车满载着猎人来到电工房。后挡板打开后,弗兰基跳了下来。猎人们读过有关它的报道,看到黄脖圈,断定它就是弗兰基。

每到捕猎季节,乔治和其他在格伦加德纳疗养中心的人就要争论,为了弗兰基的安全,是否该把它关在马厩里,这样他们自己也放心。但是每次表决结果都不赞成这么做。弗兰基象征着格伦加德纳疗养中心的创办思想——提供照看服务,但不限制自由。

"鹿和人一样,它们有自己的尊严,"简说道,"我们决不能夺走它们自己的选择。"

所以,雄鹿弗兰基,这只深受格伦加德纳中心人们钟爱的鹿,一直自由自在。当然,它也会有风险,但生活本身就是风险。而且弗兰基知道它有可以依赖的朋友。

The Shadowland of Dreams
梦的幻境

You are what your deep driving desire is,

As your desire is,so is your will.

As your will is,so is your deed.

As your deed is,so is your destiny.

Brihadaranyaka Upanishad IV.4.5

内心的渴望决定欲望；

欲望决定意愿；

意愿决定行为；

行为决定命运。

摘自《广林奥义书》(婆罗门教经典著作)第4部第4章第5节

Many a young person tells me he wants to be a writer.I always encourage such people,but I also explain that there's a big difference between "being a writer" and writing.In most cases these individuals are dreaming of wealth and fame,not the long hours alone at the type-writer. "You've got to want to write,"I say to them, "not want to be a writer."

The reality is that writing is a lonely,private and poor-paying affair.For every writer kissed by fortune,there are thousands more whose longing is never requited. Even those who succeed often know long periods of neglect and poverty.I did.

When I left a 20-year career in the Coast Guard to become a freelance writer,I had no prospects at all.What I did have was a friend with whom I'd grown up in Henning,Tennessee.George found me my home—a cleaned-out storage room in the Greenwich Village apartment building where he worked as superintendent. It didn't even matter that it was cold and had no bathroom.Immediately I bought a used manual typewriter and felt like a genuine writer.

After a year or so,however,I still hadn't received a break and began to doubt myself.It was so hard to sell a story that I barely made enough to eat.But I knew I wanted to write.I had dreamed about it for years.I wasn't going to be one of those people who die wondering, "What if?"I would keep putting my dream to the test—even though it meant living with uncertainty and fear of failure.This is the Shadow-land of hope,and anyone with a dream must learn to live there.

许多年轻人对我说他们想当作家,我总是鼓励这些人,但我也会向他们解释,写作与"当作家"之间存在着很大的差别。在多数情况下,这些人是梦想着一夜暴富、一夜成名,而没有想到要在打字机前度过的漫长而又寂寞的时光。"你们得想着写作,"我告诉他们,"而不要总想着当作家。"

事实上写作是种孤独、私密,而且收入微薄的工作。除了那些被幸运之神垂青的作家外,但成千上万人的努力和渴望却得不到回报。就算那些成功的作家也往往经历过长期的默默无闻与穷困潦倒,而我正是这样的。

在我结束了20年的海岸警卫队生涯、决心成为一名自由撰稿人的时候,我的前途一片渺茫。我所仅有的是一个和我一起在田纳西州亨宁长大的朋友。乔治帮我找了一间房子……是格林尼治村公寓一间腾空的储藏室,他在那里当门卫。那儿非常冷,而且没有盥洗室,不过没关系。我迫不及待地买了一台二手的手动打字机,感觉自己就像是一名天才作家一样。

在接下来约一年的时间里,仍没有任何时来运转的迹象,我不禁开始怀疑自己。出版作品太难了,我基本上连肚子都填不饱。但是我知道我想写,这是我多年的梦想。我可不想在弥留之际再问自己:"如果当初坚持下来会怎样?"我要检验我的梦想,即使生活在不安定与对失败的恐惧中也在所不惜。这就是所谓的"希望的虚幻境界"吧,有梦想的人就要学会活在这幻境之中。

Then one day I got a call that changed my life.It wasn't an agent or editor offering a big contract.It was the opposite—a kind of siren call tempting me to give up my dream.On the phone was an old acquaintance from the Coast Guard,now stationed in San Francisco.He had once lent me a few bucks and liked to egg me about it. "When am I going to get the $15,Alex? "he teased.

"Next time I make a sale."

"I have a better idea,"he said."We need a new public-information assistant out here,and we're paying $6,000 a year.If you want it,you can have it."

Six thousand a year! That was real money in 1960.I could get a nice apartment,a used car,pay off debts and maybe save a little something.What's more,I could write on the side.

As the dollars were dancing in my head,something cleared my senses.From deep inside a bull-headed resolution welled up.I had dreamed of being a writer—full time.And that's what I was going to be. "Thanks,but no,"I heard myself saying. "I'm going to stick it out and write."

Afterward,as I paced around my little room,I started to feel like a fool.Reaching into my cupboard—an orange crate nailed to the wall— I pulled out all that was there:two cans of sardines.Plunging my hands in my pockets,I came up with 18 cents.I took the cans and coins and jammed them into a crumpled paper bag.There Alex,I said to myself.There's everything you've made of yourself so far.I'm not sure I ever felt so low.

I wish I could say things started getting better right away.But they didn't.Thank goodness I had George to help me over the rough spots.

Through him I met other struggling artists,like Joe Delaney,a veteran painter from Knoxville,Tennessee.Often Joe lacked food money,so he'd visit a neighborhood butcher who would give him big bones with morsels of meat,and a grocer who would hand him some wilted vegetables.That's all Joe needed to make down-home soup.

有一天,我接到一个改变了我一生的电话。不是出版中介或者编辑有大的合同要和我签,恰恰相反,而是像海上女妖莎琳(译者注:半人半鸟的海妖,常用歌声诱惑过路的航海者而使航船触礁毁灭)般来诱惑我放弃我的梦想。来电话的是我在海岸警卫队的一位老熟人,现在驻扎在旧金山。他曾借给我一些钱,喜欢借此挖苦我。他揶揄道,"亚历克斯,我什么时候能要回我那15美元?"

"下次等我卖了一篇稿子后。"

"我倒有个好主意,"他说道,"我们这里需要一位公共信息助理,工资6 000美元一年,如果你想干,这个工作就是你的啦。"

年薪6 000美元!在1960年,这个数目的确不小。我可以住上好公寓,弄一辆二手车,还清我所有的债务,也许还能有点存款。而且,我可以一边工作一边写作。

当钞票在我脑袋里翩翩起舞的时候,有什么东西使我马上清醒过来。一股牛脾气从内心深处爆发。我一直梦想成为一名作家——全职的,这才是我所追求的。我听见自己这么说:"谢谢,但是不用了,我要撑下去,继续写作。"

接完电话后,我在我那间局促的屋里踱着步,觉得自己太傻了。我从碗柜(其实就是钉在墙上的装橘子的柳条箱)中拿出了里面所有的东西……两罐沙丁鱼罐头。我搜遍了所有的口袋,就只有18美分了。我把罐头和硬币全塞进一个皱巴巴的纸袋里,然后对自己说:亚历克斯,这就是你目前为止所有的财产了……我不清楚是否还有比这更落魄的时候了。

我希望我能说情况马上就要有好转了,但事情并不是这样子的。谢天谢地!我有乔治帮我渡过难关。

通过他我结识了其他在困境中挣扎的艺术家,比如乔·德莱尼,他是一位从田纳西州诺克斯维尔来的老画家。当乔没钱吃饭的时候,他就会去找附近的屠夫要些带肉的大骨头,找杂货店老板要些打蔫的蔬菜,这样乔就可以熬一锅南方风味的汤了。

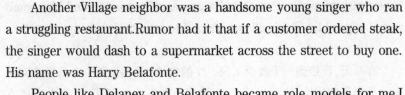

Another Village neighbor was a handsome young singer who ran a struggling restaurant.Rumor had it that if a customer ordered steak, the singer would dash to a supermarket across the street to buy one. His name was Harry Belafonte.

People like Delaney and Belafonte became role models for me.I learned that you had to make sacrifices and live creatively to keep working at your dreams.That's what living in the Shadowland is all about.

As I absorbed the lesson,I gradually began to sell my articles.I was writing about what many people were talking about then:civil rights,black Americans and Africa.Soon,like birds flying south,my thoughts were drawn back to my childhood.In the silence of my room,I heard the voices of Grandma,Cousin Georgia,Aunt Plus,Aunt Liz and Aunt Till as they told stories about our family and slavery.

These were stories that black Americans had tended to avoid before,and so I mostly kept them to myself.But one day at lunch with editors of *Reader's Digest*,I told these stories of my grandmother and aunts and cousins.I said that I had a dream to trace my family's history to the first African brought to these shores in chains.I left that lunch with a contract that would help support my research and writing for nine years.

It was a long,slow climb out of the shadows.Yet in 1970,17 years after I left the Coast Guard,*Roots* was published.Instantly I had the kind of fame and success that few writers ever experience.The shadows had turned into dazzling limelight.

For the first time I had money and open doors everywhere.The phone rang all the time with new friends and new deals.I packed up and moved to Los Angeles,where I could help in the making of the *Roots* TV mini-series.It was a confusing,exhilarating time,and in a sense,I was blinded by the light of my success.

Then one day,while unpacking,I came across a box filled with things I had owned years before in the Village.Inside was a brown paper bag.

I opened it,and there were two corroded sardine cans,a nickel,a

格林尼治村另一位街坊是一位年轻英俊的歌手，他勉强维持着一家小餐馆。据传如果客人点了一份牛排，他就会冲到马路对面超市去买一份,他的名字叫哈里·贝拉方特。

德莱尼和贝拉方特这些人为我树立了榜样，从他们那儿我明白你要为实现梦想而做出牺牲、创造性地生活。"幻境"中的生活就是这样。

明白这个道理的同时,我也逐渐开始发表了一些文章。我写的都是那时一些热门话题……什么人权啦、美国黑人啦、非洲啦。很快我的思绪就像南飞的小鸟一样飞回了我的童年。在我寂静的房间里,我仿佛听到了奶奶的声音,乔治亚表哥、普卢斯婶婶、利兹婶婶、蒂尔婶婶的声音,他们正说着关于我们家族和奴隶制的故事。

以前美国黑人倾向于回避这些故事，所以大部分我都深深地埋在心底。但是一天在和《读者文摘》的编辑们一起吃午饭的时候,我给他们讲了这些我的祖母、姊姊和表哥的故事。我说我有一个梦想,就是追寻家族的足迹去寻找那第一个带着枷锁来到这边海岸的非洲人。午餐结束后,我带着一份足可支持我研究写作9年之久的合同离开了。

我用了很长的时间才冲破成功前的漫长黑暗。那是1970年,也就是我离开海岸警卫队的17年后,我的作品《根》出版了,我立刻就拥有了很少作家才能体验到的名望与成功。终于,黑暗变成了炫目的聚光灯。

平生第一次我有钱了,而且各地的大门都向我敞开。电话响个不停,给我带来新朋友、新合约。我整理行装,搬到洛杉矶去居住,在那里我可以协助《根》的小型电视连续剧的拍摄。那真是一段令人迷乱又振奋人心的时光。而且从某种意义上说,我被成功的光芒蒙蔽了双眼。

后来有一天,我在拆打包的行李时,偶然发现了一个盒子,里面全是多年前我在格林尼治村的东西,其中有一个棕色的纸袋。

我把它打开,里面是两罐生锈的沙丁鱼罐头,一枚10分、一枚5分、3枚

dime and three pennies.Suddenly the past came flooding in like a rip-tide.I could picture myself once again huddled over the typewriter in that cold,bleak,one-room apartment.And I said to myself,*The things in this bag are part of my roots,too.I can't ever forget that.*

I sent them out to be framed in Lucite.I keep that clear plastic case where I can see it every day.I can see it now above my office desk in Knoxville,along with the Pulitzer Prize,a portrait of nine Emmys awarded to the TV production of *Roots*,and the Spingarn medal—the NAACP's highest honor.I'd be hard pressed to say which means the most to me.But only one reminds me of the courage and persistence it takes to stay the course in the Shadowland.

It's a lesson anyone with a dream should learn.

Alex Haley

1分的硬币。突然之间,往事如潮水般涌上心头,我能想象过去的我蜷在寒冷凄清的单间里、伏在打字机前工作的情景。于是我对自己说,这个袋子里的东西也是我的"根"的一部分,我永远不能将它遗忘。

我让人用透明合成树脂给它们镶给了个框。我把这个塑料盒子放在我每天都能看见的地方。现在它就摆在我诺克斯维尔的办公室桌上。旁边还摆着普利策新闻奖(译者注:美国的一种在文学、艺术和新闻界内颁发的奖),电视剧《根》曾获得的9个艾美奖(译者注:美国电视艺术和科学学会每年颁发给在电视节目上有突出成就者的奖)的纪念照片。还有斯平加恩勋章——美国全国有色人种进步协会最高荣誉。这让我无法说清哪一个奖对我更重要。但它时常提醒我,要在阴影下坚持自己的道路需要多大的勇气和毅力。

这是每个有梦想的人必修的一课。

The Magic Bat
魔法球棒

You may be disappointed if you fail,but you are doomed if you don't try.

Beverly Sills

失败也许会令你灰心,但若是不去尝试,你就注定会失败。

贝弗利·希尔斯

Harry is every coach's dream kid:He shows up for every practice early,stays late and is enthusiastic.Harry is also every coach's nightmare:He has neither the instinct nor the physical talent for the game.

I stepped in as a stand-in coach for my son's Little League team when the regular coach got married.Somehow he thought a honeymoon took precedence over next Tuesday's game.How can you blame him?Our team hadn't won in more than two years.

As I accepted the fill-in spot,I promised myself that I would show no disappointment if we lost.That was the least I could do.The

哈里是所有教练都梦寐以求的孩子:每一次训练他总是来得早,走得迟,而且练得很积极。但他也是教练的噩梦:他缺乏运动天赋,也没有打棒球所需的身体素质。

我儿子所在的"小小联盟队"教练请婚假时,我去担任了临时教练。不知为什么,这位教练把他的蜜月放在了下周二的一场比赛前面。但你又怎能说他呢?两年多来我们队从未赢过。

当初我接受当临时教练的任务时,就暗下了决心:如果我们队输了,我不能流露出半点失望的情绪。最少我也能做到这一点。要说我所能做的

best I could do was give a good heart to the effort.

I met Harry at the first practice.A small,thin awkward kid,his best throw was about five feet,which made the choice of fielding position difficult.And he was scared.Every time he came to bat,he would glance at the pitcher,lean the bat on his shoulder,close his eyes and wait until the misery of three pitches was over.Then he'd trudge back to the dugout.It was painful to watch.

I met Harry before Tuesday's game,took him aside and worked with him on keeping his eyes open.He tried,but it's tough to overcome the habit of fear.We were about to play a team that had beat us 22-1 the last time.It didn't seem a fortunate moment for a breakthrough.Then I thought,*Why not?*

I went to the dugout,got a different bat and returned to our practice area. "Harry,"I said, "I want you to use this bat.It's the one for you.It's a magic bat.All you have to do is swing and it will hit the ball."

Harry seemed skeptical,but he said he would try.I hoped I wasn't complicating an already tough problem for Harry,but I wanted to try to help.

Our team was trailing from the first inning.No surprise in that,but we had some loyal parents in the stands to give constant encouragement to the kids.

On Harry's first at bat,I noticed he wasn't using his special bat, but I didn't step in.He struck out,as usual,and I decided to let it ride.

We were able to score from time to time.In the last inning,we were behind by only three runs.I was thinking about a "respectable outcome" speech to give the kids while packing up the gear.As the home team,we were last up.We alternated for five batters between singles with players safely on base and strikeouts.We had bases loaded and two outs.Only then did I notice that Harry was our last chance.

Surveying the field from my spot by first base,I saw the left fielder sprawl on the grass as Harry came from the dugout.He obviously expected no action.The right fielder was bothering some butter-

最多的，该是对孩子们的努力好好鼓励一番。

第一次训练时我见到了哈里。哈里是个又瘦又小、举止笨拙的孩子，他最好的投球纪录是5英尺，在这个距离上很难选好接球位置。不仅如此，哈里胆子还很小。每次到他击球时，他就匆匆瞥一眼投手，把球棒靠在肩膀上，接着闭上眼睛等待神奇的3次投球结束。然后经过长途跋涉回到队员席。看他比赛确实很痛苦。

礼拜二的比赛前，我找了哈里，我把他叫到一边做工作，让他一定把眼睛睁开。他尝试了一下，不过要完全克服这个习惯很难。我们的对手上次曾以22:1赢了我们，这次想要做个突破的话谈何容易！不过转念一想，又有什么不能呢？

我去队员席另拿了一只球棒，回到了比赛区。"哈里，"我说，"我想让你用这只球棒。这是专门给你的。这是一只有魔力的球棒。你只管使劲挥，它准能击中球。"

哈里将信将疑，但答应试试。比赛对哈里来说已经够难的了，我暗自希望，我没有给他增加负担。但我很想对他能有所帮助。

第一局结束了，我们队无精打采地走下场。这完全在我的意料之中，好在观众席上我们还有些忠实的家长们给孩子们鼓劲。

我注意到哈里击球时并未用我给他的专用球棒，但我没有去干涉他。跟往常一样，他三击出局了，我想随他去吧。

我们队不时得分。最后一局时，我们只落后了3分。我一边收拾东西，一边已经在准备就今天"非常体面的比赛结果"跟孩子们说点什么。作为主场队，我们已经干得很不错了。这时我才突然意识到要想赢，哈里是我们唯一的机会了。

纵观球场，从我的位置到一垒处，我看见哈里从队员席走出时，左边的守场员懒洋洋地躺在草地上。很明显，他觉得哈里不会有什么动作。右

fly that was flitting about.The shortstop had moved well in,I suppose anticipating the possibility of a miraculous bunt.Clearly,the opposing players were already tasting the double-scoop ice cream cones they would go for after the victory.

Harry limped up to the batter's box.I noticed he had his usual bat.I called a time out,ran up to him and whispered,"Harry,this is the time for the magic bat.Give it a try.Just keep your eyes open and swing."

He looked at me in disbelief,but he said he'd try.He walked off for the special bat as I trotted back to first base.

First pitch,strike one.Harry didn't swing,but he kept his eyes open.I pumped my fist and gave it a little swing,encouraging him to swing.He smiled,got into his awkward stance and waited.He swung, eyes open,but missed.Strike two.That was the first real swing Harry had ever taken.Who cared if we won the game?I considered Harry a winner already.

The other coach yelled to his pitcher,"Fire one past him and end this thing! "I grimaced.

The pitcher threw a straight fastball and Harry swung.The magic bat did its trick.It found the ball,which flew over the shortstop's head.

Pandemonium erupted in the stands,in the dugouts,on the bases.I was cheering Harry to run to first as fast as he could.It seemed like an eternity.The left fielder called to the center fielder to get it."You're closer! "

I kept cheering the runners.We had one in at home and three guys pouring it on from first to second,second to third,third to home. The second baseman yelled for the center fielder to get the ball to him.Excitedly,he obeyed,but the ball skipped across the grass and passed by the second baseman toward the right-field line.My job as

双语精华版心灵鸡汤 ·

coach was simple at this point."Run,guys,run,"I yelled.

Another guy scored.By this time,the entire team had joined the cheering, "Go,Harry,go,Harry! "This was surely the longest distance

边的守场员此时正被飞来飞去的蝴蝶弄得心烦意乱。游击手已移动到场地中间,我想他一定准备好了接个漂亮的触击球。现在形势十分清楚,对方队员庆祝胜利的两球冰激凌已经差不多到嘴了。

哈里蹒跚走到了击球员区。我注意到他拿的是他平常用的球棒。我叫了暂停,跑到他跟前耳语道:"哈里,现在是用魔法球棒的时候了,试试看,只要睁开眼睛挥棒就行。"

哈里怀疑地看着我,答应去试试。他转身去拿那只球棒,而我则小跑回到一垒处。

第一投,哈里第一击。这次他并未使劲挥击,但他一直睁着眼睛。我握起拳头轻轻挥动,鼓励他要使劲挥臂。他笑了,恢复了他一贯显得笨拙的站姿,等待着。第二击,哈里挥动球棒,睁大双眼,但却没有击中。这是哈里第一次将挥击的动作做到位。比赛是否能赢已经不重要,我认为哈里已经胜利了。

对方的教练对他们的投手大喊:"来个狠的,让他接不住,结束比赛!"我皱起了眉头。

投手投出了一个直线快球,哈里振臂一挥,这次魔法球棒显灵了,球从游击手头上飞过,被球棒击中了。

观众席、队员席、垒区的人们都骚动起来。哈里以他的最快速度向一垒跑去,我使劲为他加油。这一刻似乎长得无穷无尽。左边的守场员朝游击手大喊,让他上去接球,"你离得更近些!"

我一直在给场上队员鼓劲。现在我们本垒里有1个人,3个人正从一垒跑向二垒,二垒跑向三垒,三垒跑向本垒。第二垒的球手朝中间的守场员大喊,让他抢到球传给自己。中场队员确实想这么做,无奈球飞过草地,从第二垒的队员身边掠过,朝右边线飞过去。这时,身为教练,我的任务十分简单:"快跑,伙计们,加油!"我大喊着。

又一个队员得分了。这时全队都加入了加油的行列。"哈里,加油,加

生命的彩虹

Harry had ever run.He was panting as he headed for third and another guy crossed home.

The right fielder's throw was critical,and it was pretty good,but the third baseman muffed it.The ball scooted past him out of play. The rule:one base on an overthrow that goes out of play.Harry, exhausted,kept the push on as best as he could.

About then,the first cry of "Grand Slam! "hit the air.Everyone joined in.When Harry reached home plate,about to collapse,his team- mates lifted him as high as they could and chanted, "Harry,Harry, Harry! "

I ran over to the team to hug the proudest kid in America.Tears streaming,Harry looked up at me and said,"The bat,Coach,the bat."

I smiled and said,"No,Harry.It was you who hit the ball,not the bat."

David Meanor

Submitted by Don "Ollie" Olivett

油!"这准是哈里跑过的最长的距离。他气喘吁吁地跑向第三垒时,另一个队员穿过了本垒。

右边守场员的一投十分关键,球投得很漂亮,但三垒的队员失误了,球从他身边掠过,落在了场外。根据比赛规则,球落在场外的一方为负。而哈里这时已经筋疲力尽了,仍在坚持往前跑。

此时此刻,场上蓦然响起一声欢呼!随后每个人都加入了进来。当哈里终于跑回到本队中时,已经快要瘫了。队员们把哈里高高抛起,一起叫着:"哈里! 哈里! 哈里! "

我向队员们跑去,紧紧拥抱这个争气的孩子。哈里噙着两行热泪,抬头看着我说道:"球棒,教练,球棒! "

我微笑道:"不,哈里,是你击中了球,不是那个魔法球棒。"

Attitude is Everything
态度决定一切

Jerry was the kind of guy you love to hate.He was always in a good mood and always had something positive to say.When someone would ask him how he was doing,he would reply,"If I were any better,I would be twins！"

He was a unique manager because he had several waiters who had followed him around from restaurant to restaurant.The reason the waiters followed Jerry was because of his attitude.He was a natural motivator.If an employee was having a bad day,Jerry was there telling the employee how to look on the positive side of the situation.

Seeing this style really made me curious,so one day I went up to Jerry and asked him,"I don't get it！You can't be a positive,up person all the time.How do you do it？"

Jerry replied,"Each morning I wake up and say to myself,'Jerry you have two choices today.You can choose to be in a good mood or

杰瑞是那种容易招人嫉恨的人。他心情总是很好,总有一些积极的、乐观的话要说。如果有人问他觉得怎么样,他一定会回答:"如果我能更好的话,那就是说我是双胞胎！"

他是个很独特的餐厅经理。他手下有一批服务生,无论他到哪一家餐厅工作,他们都跟着他。他们愿意跟着他,主要是因为他的开朗态度。他是一个十分自然的激励人心,鼓舞斗志的人;如果哪个员工日子不顺,心情不好,杰瑞总会告诉他,如何以乐观的态度来看待事情。

他的这种行事作风使我很好奇, 有一天我终于问他:"我不懂你怎么能永远保持乐观、开朗的态度,你是怎么做到的？"

杰瑞回答道:"每天早上我醒来时都告诉自己,'杰瑞, 你今天有两种

生命的彩虹

199

you can choose to be in a bad mood.'I choose to be in a good mood. Each time something bad happens,I can choose to be a victim or I can choose to learn from it.I choose to learn from it.Every time someone comes to me complaining,I can choose to accept their complaining or I can point out the positive side of life.I choose the positive side of life."

"Yeah,right,it's not that easy,"I protested.

"Yes it is,"Jerry said. "Life is all about choices.When you cut away all the junk,every situation is a choice.You choose how you react to situations.You choose how people will affect your mood.You choose to be in a good or bad mood.The bottom line:it's your choice how you live life."

I reflected on what Jerry said.Soon thereafter,I left the restaurant industry to start my own business.We lost touch,but I often thought about him when I made a choice about life instead of reacting to it.

Several years later,I heard that Jerry did something you are never supposed to do in the restaurant business:he left the back door open one morning and was held up at gunpoint by three armed robbers. While trying to open the safe,his hand,shaking from nervousness, slipped off the combination.The robbers panicked and shot him. Luckily,Jerry was found relatively quickly and rushed to the local trauma center.After 18 hours of surgery and weeks of intensive care, Jerry was released from the hospital with fragments of the bullets still in his body.

I saw Jerry about six months after the accident.When I asked him how he was,he replied, "If I were any better,I'd be twins.Wanna see my scars? "I declined to see his wounds,but did ask him what had gone through his mind as the robbery took place.

"The first thing that went through my mind was that I should have locked the back door,"Jerry replied. "Then,as I lay on the floor,I remembered that I had two choices:I could choose to live,or I could choose to die.I chose to live."

"Weren't you scared? Did you lose consciousness? "I asked.

选择,你可以选择有好心情,也可以选择有坏心情。'我当然选择好心情。每次有什么不好的事情发生的时候,我可以选择甘当受害者,也可以选择从中汲取教训,于是我就选择汲取教训;每次有人到我这里抱怨,我可以选择接受他们的抱怨,也可以选择替他们指出生命的光明面,于是我选择指出光明面。"

"是啊,很对,可是事情没这么简单吧。"我提出异议。

"事情就是这么简单,"杰瑞说,"生命的全部意义就是一次次的抉择。把所有无关紧要的东西去除掉后,每种情形就是一次选择。你可以选择如何面对这些情形,可以选择要不要让人来影响你的心情,更可以选择要有好心情或坏心情。底线就在于:你要如何过日子,完全是你自己的选择。"

我反复揣摩杰瑞的话。不久之后,我就离开餐饮业,另起炉灶,开创自己的事业。我和杰瑞失去了联络,但每当我在面对生活做抉择时,常常会想到他,而非只对这种选择一筹莫展。

几年后,我听说杰瑞由于一时疏忽铸成餐饮界不可饶恕的错误:有天,他忘了关后门,结果凌晨有3个歹徒持枪闯进来,用枪指着他,叫他打开保险箱。他在开保险箱时,因为紧张过度,双手颤抖,错过了密码,结果歹徒在惊慌之下,便开枪杀他。幸运的是,他及时被发现,医护人员将他紧急送往当地医疗中心。经过18个小时的手术,并在重病特护室待了好几个星期后,杰瑞总算平安出院,但体内还残留着子弹的碎片。

那次事件6个月后,我遇见杰瑞。我问他觉得怎么样,他回答:"如果我能更好的话,那就是说我是双胞胎!你要不要看看我的伤疤?"我婉言拒绝了看他伤口的建议,我只是问他,抢案发生的当时,他心里到底是怎么想的。

"我当时第一件想到的事情,就是我应该把后门锁好,"杰瑞这样回答,"后来我倒在地板上的时候,我又想起我有两种选择:一种是生,一种是死。我选择了生。"

"你不害怕吗?你有没有失去知觉?"我问。

Jerry continued,"The paramedics were great.They kept telling me I was going to be fine.But when they wheeled me into the emergency room and I saw the expressions on the faces of the doctors and nurses, I got really scared.In their eyes,I read, 'He's a dead man.'I knew I needed to take action."

"What did you do？"I asked.

"Well,there was a big,burly nurse shouting questions at me,"said Jerry."She asked if I was allergic to anything.'Yes,'I replied.The doctors and nurses stopped working as they waited for my reply.I took a deep breath and yelled,'Bullets！'Over their laughter,I told them,'I am choosing to live.Operate on me as if I am alive,not dead.'"

Jerry lived thanks to the skill of his doctors,but also because of his amazing attitude.I learned from him that every day we have the choice to live fully.Attitude,after all,is everything.

Francie Baltazar-Schwartz

杰瑞继续说:"那些急救人员很棒,他们一再告诉我,我一定会平安无事的。但是等他们把我推进急诊室,我一看到那些医生、护士脸上的表情,心里马上凉了半截,开始害怕起来,因为他们的眼神仿佛在说:'这是个死人。'于是我知道自己必须采取行动。"

"你采取了什么行动?"我问。

"呃,当时有个很高大、很健壮的护士慌慌张张地大声问我,有没有对什么东西过敏,'有,'我回答,所有的医生、护士都停下手上的动作,等着我的答案。我深深吸了一口气,然后大叫道:'对子弹过敏!'他们大笑过后,我就告诉他们:'我要活下去!动手术的时候,把我当成活人,不要把我当成死人。'"

杰瑞能活下来,一方面固然要归功于医生的高明技术,另一方面也是出于他自己令人惊异的态度。我从他身上彻底领悟,每天我们都可以选择活得充实愉快。毕竟,态度决定一切。

Airport Dining
难忘的机场晚餐

There are no days in life so memorable as those
which vibrated to some stroke of the imagination.

Ralph Waldo Emerson

一生中没有比那些能激发想象力的日子更让人
记忆深刻的了。

拉尔夫·沃尔朵·爱默生

Several years ago,as I was looking over my travel itinerary for a business trip from San Francisco to New Orleans,I noticed that I would have some time at the airport in Dallas before catching my connecting flight.

So I called my friend Luke who lives in Dallas,and said,"Luke,I've got an hour-and-a-half layover at the airport.If you'll come out and meet my plane,I'll treat you to dinner."

Luke enthusiastically agreed,and I was excited by the prospect of getting to spend a little time with him.

When the pilot announced that our flight would be delayed on the ground an extra few minutes in San Francisco because of air

几年前,当我查阅从旧金山到新奥尔良出公差的行程安排时,我注意到在达拉斯机场转机的间隙,有一段自由支配的时间。

于是,我打电话给住在达拉斯的朋友卢克说:"卢克,我要在达拉斯机场转机,中间有一个半小时的时间。如果你来接我,我请你吃晚饭。"

卢克热情地答应了,一想到能和他小聚,我也激动不已。

当飞行员宣布由于空中交通管制,飞机将在旧金山机场推迟几分钟

生命的彩虹

203

traffic control I paid no attention,but as those few minutes dragged on,I became more agitated and upset.Every minute that passed was one minute less that I would be able to spend with my friend.

The pilot promised to make up the lost time en route,but he wasn't able to do so.The plane arrived in Dallas an hour late. That left me only half an hour to visit with Luke,and I still needed time to catch my connecting flight.At this point,I knew that our having dinner together was totally out of the question.The Dallas-Fort Worth airport is too big;thirty minutes is barely enough time to dash from one plane to the next.

When I stepped off the plane,Luke was there,waiting for me.

"Hey,Luke,"I said apologetically,"thanks for coming out to meet me.I hope you didn't have to wait here too long."

"Oh,no problem,"he replied easily."I called ahead and found out your plane was going to be late."

"Oh,good,"I replied,distracted by the time pressure. "Look,I'm really sorry about dinner,but I'll owe you one next time.Come on,we-'ll find out what gate my next plane is leaving from.We can head over there together and talk a bit."

I started walking but Luke didn't budge.

"I am very invested in having dinner with you,"he said to me.

I looked back at him incredulously. "What are you talking about?"I laughed. "The only way you're going to have dinner with me tonight is if you buy a plane ticket to New Orleans! "

"We're having dinner,"replied Luke with determination. "Believe me,I have this whole thing scoped out..Just follow me."

He picked up one of my bags and carried it out through the se-curity check.I followed him closely,silently protesting and growing more anxious with every passing moment.He started running,down into the parking garage,and I ran along behind him,thinking to myself,

双语精华版心灵鸡汤·

204

There is no way we are going to get into his car,drive to a restaurant, have dinner,and still get back in time for me to make my plane!

The two of us hustled down a short flight of stairs in the parking garage and walked rapidly along several rows of cars until we came to the place where Luke's car was parked.I immediately noticed that

起飞时,我并未在意。但随着这几分钟的时间一再拖延,我变得越来越烦躁不安。因为每过去一分钟,就意味着我和朋友见面的时间要少一分钟。

飞行员保证在飞行途中补回损失的时间,但是他最终没能补回来。飞机到达拉斯时晚点了1个小时。这样一来,我和卢克只能有半个小时的时间聊天了,而且,我还要转机。所以,我估计和卢克共进晚餐看来是彻底没有可能了。

当我走下飞机时,卢克正站在人群中等我呢。

"嗨,卢克,"我满怀歉意地说,"谢谢你来接我,希望没让你等太久。"

"哦,没关系,"他轻松地答道。"我提前打了电话,知道飞机晚点。"

"噢,那就好,"我回答说,被紧迫的时间搞得心烦意乱。"嗯,抱歉今天不能请你吃晚饭了,下次一定补上。快点儿,我们去找转机口。我们边走边聊吧。"

说完,我向前走去,但卢克却站在那里纹丝不动。

"我可是非常想和你一起吃晚饭啊,"他对我说。

我疑惑地回头看着他,笑道:"你说什么呢?除非你也买一张飞往新奥尔良的机票,我们今天才能共进晚餐!"

"我们这就去吃晚餐,"卢克果断地答道。"相信我,我已经全都安排好了,你就跟我走吧。"

他说着拎起我的一个包径直向前走去,过了安检。我只能紧紧地跟在他后面,心里暗暗埋怨他,并且随着时间一分一秒地流逝,我越来越感到焦急。这时,他跑了起来,进了多层停车库,而我则跟在他后面跑着,心想:"现在要坐他的车去饭店吃晚餐,再返回来赶飞机,这简直是不可能!"

我们飞快地跑下多层停车库的一小段楼梯,然后又迅速地穿过好几排汽车,才来到卢克的汽车前面。这时,我立刻发现在他汽车旁边的停车

in the parking space next to his car,he had set up a folding table.

Luke pulled out his car keys and opened the trunk of his car.He reached in and pulled out a checkered picnic tablecloth,which he spread with a grand flourish over the table.Then he grabbed two folding chairs and set them up next to the table.Then a bottle of champagne and a large container of hors d'oeuvres.He set a candle in the center of the table and lit it.We popped the champagne and broke out the hors d'oeuvres.

There we were,sitting across the table from each other in the middle of a parking lot,toasting each other with champagne and grinning from ear to ear.Carbon monoxide fumes may have been swirling all around us,but we didn't care.Drivers in search of a parking place were annoyed at us for taking up the space,but once they took a closer look,many of them broke into astonished smiles.

With seven and one-half minutes to go,we put everything back in the trunk and ran for my plane.We readily got through the security check and arrived back at Gate 23 with five minutes to spare.What Luke and I had not remembered,however,was that my next flight was leaving from Gate 31,which was in the other terminal! There was no way I was going to get from Terminal 2 to Terminal 3 in time to make my plane.

I was starting to get hysterical.But Luke was ready for anything—he flagged down an airport employee who was driving an electric cart,and we jumped on the back.

"Our plane is leaving from Gate 31 in three minutes! "Luke implored.

The driver was up to the challenge.He drove the cart like a Grand Prix racer,dodging and weaving around the pedestrians.We loudly applauded his every move.We were laughing.We were screaming.We were cheering him on.

We arrived at the gate with only seconds to spare.The entire area was deserted except for one last flight attendant.She had spotted us in the distance,as our vehicle careened madly toward her gate.I leapt off,yelling,"Can I still make this plane?I need to get on this plane! "

The flight attendant scolded me,in mock anger."Where have you

位上,他早就已经摆好了一张折叠桌。

卢克掏出车钥匙,打开了汽车的后备箱,从里面拿出了一块野餐用的方格桌布,潇洒地将其展开铺在桌子上。接着,他又拽出两把折叠椅展开在桌旁。然后,是一瓶香槟酒和一大罐餐前开胃菜。接着,他在桌子中央点上了一根蜡烛。我们打开那瓶香槟酒并把开胃菜放好。

就这样,在停车场中央,我们面对面地坐着,互敬着香槟,开心地笑着。我们也许陷落于浓烈的一氧化碳气体之中,但是我们毫不在意。不过,这可惹恼了那些找位置停车的司机了,因为我们占了停车位。然而当他们驶近看清楚之后,许多人都惊讶地笑了。

离飞机起飞只剩7分半钟的时候,我们把所有东西都收进后备箱,便撒开腿跑去赶飞机。当我们迅速地通过安检回到23号登机门时,距离飞机起飞仅剩下5分钟了。但是,我和卢克竟然忘了我要转乘的那趟航班是在31号入口登机,是在另外一个候机楼!要知道在5分钟的时间里,从第二候机楼赶到第三候机楼再登上飞机,这是根本不可能的!

这时,我快急疯了。但是,卢克好像早有准备似的,他招手拦下一位驾驶电动车的机场职员,接着我和他一起跳上车的后部。

"我们的飞机还有3分钟就要从31号登机口起飞了! "卢克恳求道。

这位司机立刻接受了这严峻的挑战。他把车开得像参加国际汽车大奖赛似的,左突右冲,躲避着过往的行人,我们不禁一次又一次地为他大声鼓掌欢呼。就这样,一路上,我们笑着、叫着,不停地为他喝彩。

当我们赶到登机处的时候,离起飞时间只剩下几秒钟了。整个登机口除了一个跟班乘务员外,见不到任何人影。她老远就瞧见我们,我们的车横冲直撞地冲向登机口。我跳下车,大声说:"我仍能赶上这趟班机吗?我要上飞机。"

been?You think we can wait all day for you?Get on this plane right now! "

She grabbed my ticket,rushed me on board and slammed the door behind me.I collapsed into my seat,relieved and energized by the whole bizarre experience.

Throughout the entire flight,images of my dinner with Luke popped into my head.But then I realized the whole thing had happened so quickly that I hadn't really had a chance to thank him properly.

So as soon as the plane landed I called him at home and said, "Luke,that was such a wonderful thing you did for me.I really want to thank you."

"You don't have to thank me,"Luke replied evenly. "Somebody already beat you to it."

"What are you talking about?"I asked.

"When I got back to my car,"he explained, "there was a flower on the windshield,with a little note that said:Anybody who would do something like that for another person must be a beautiful human being."

Matt Weinstein

乘务员故作生气地厉声责备道："你刚才干吗去啦？你以为我们会在这儿为你等上一整天啊？赶快上去！"

她一把夺过我的机票，催促我上了飞机，然后"砰"的一声关上了舱门。我瘫坐在自己的座位上，长长地舒了一口气，刚才的奇妙经历使我心情激动，仍然意犹未尽。

在整个飞行过程中，我和卢克共进晚餐的情景仍历历在目。但是，我忽然意识到，整件事情发生得太快了，我竟然没有机会感谢他。

因此，飞机一着陆，我就立即给卢克家打电话："卢克，你为我所做的一切真是太棒了！我真的非常感谢你！"

"你不必感谢我，"卢克平静地答道。"已经有人代劳了。"

"你说的是什么意思？"我问道。

"当我回到车上时，"他解释道，"我发现挡风玻璃上有一枝花，还夹了一张小纸条，上面写着：一个愿意为他人做这样事情的人一定是一个心灵美好的人！"

A Lady Named Lill
有位女士名叫莉莲

Kind words can be short and easy to speak,but their echoes are truly endless.

Mother Teresa

仁慈的话语虽然简短而且很容易说出口，但它们的影响却是无限深远。

特蕾莎修女

Lillian was a young French Canadian girl who grew up in the farming community of River Canard,Ontario.At the age of 16,her father thought "Lill" had had enough schooling,and she was forced to drop out of school to contribute to the family income.In 1922,with English as her second Language and limited education and skills,the future didn't look bright for Lill.

Her father,Eugene Bezaire,was a stern man who rarely took no for an answer and never accepted excuses.He demanded that Lill find a job.But her limitations left her with little confidence and low self-esteem,and she didn't know what work she could do.

With small hope of gaining employment,she would still ride the bus daily into the "big cities" of Windsor or Detroit.But she couldn't muster the courage to respond to a Help Wanted ad;she couldn't even bring herself to knock on a door.Each day she would just ride to the city,walk aimlessly about and at dusk return home.Her father would ask,"Any luck today,Lill？"

"No...no luck today,Dad,"she would respond meekly.

As the days passed,Lill continued to ride and her father continued to ask about her job-hunting.The questions became more demanding, and Lill knew she would soon have to knock on a door.

On one of her trips,Lill saw a sign at the Carhartt Overall Company in downtown Detroit."HELP WANTED,"the sign said,"SECRE-TARIAL. APPLY WITHIN."

She walked up the long flight of stairs to the Carhartt Company offices.Cautiously,Lill knocked on her very first door.She was met by the office manager,Margaret Costello.In her broken English,Lill told

莉莲是个年轻的法裔加拿大女孩,从小生活在安大略湖(译者注:北美洲中东部介于美国和加拿大之间的湖)卡纳尔德农业小社区。16岁那年,莉莲的父亲认为她书已经读够了,于是她被迫退学了,赚钱贴补家用。1922年,莉莲除了母语外,只会一点英语,学历和技能都让人觉得捉襟见肘,前途看来不大光明。

她的父亲尤金·博扎伊尔是个很严厉的人,不但很少接受否定的答案,而且绝不接受任何借口。他要求莉莲一定要找个工作,但有限的学历让莉莲没什么信心,加上自尊心也弱,她不知道自己能做什么样的工作。

虽然她不抱什么被雇用的希望,莉莲还是每天搭公共汽车到温莎或底特律等"大城市"去。只是她鼓不起勇气,不敢按照招聘启事去找工作——她连敲人家的门都不敢。她只是每天坐车到城里,毫无头绪地四处乱逛,等天黑了再坐车回家。她父亲会问:"今天有什么运气吗,莉莲?"

"不……没什么运气,爸。"她会这样温顺地回答。

日子一天天过去,莉莲继续乘坐车子往返,她父亲继续询问她找工作的情况。不过问话的口气越来越严厉,莉莲知道自己不久就得被迫去敲人家的门了。

有一天,莉莲到城里去,她在底特律市中心的卡尔特服装公司门口看见一个招牌,上面写着:"招聘秘书,应聘者请进"。

她走过长长的楼梯,来到卡尔特服装公司办公室门口,然后小心翼翼地伸手去敲第一个门。接待她的是公司经理玛格丽特·科斯特洛,莉莲用很蹩脚的英文告诉她,自己对秘书工作很感兴趣。她还把自己的年龄说

her she was interested in the secretarial position,falsely stating that she was 19.Margaret knew something wasn't right,but decided to give the girl a chance.

She guided Lill through the old business office of the Carhartt Company.With rows and rows of people seated at rows and rows of typewriters and adding machines,Lill felt as if a hundred pairs of eyes were staring at her.With her chin on her chest and her eyes staring down,the reluctant farm girl followed Margaret to the back of the somber room.Margaret sat her down at a typewriter and said, "Lill, let's see how good you really are."

She directed Lill to type a single letter,and then left.Lill looked at the clock and saw that it was 11:40 A.M..Everyone would be leaving for lunch at noon.She figured that she could slip away in the crowd then.But she knew she should at least attempt the letter.

On her first try,she got through one line.It had five words,and she made four mistakes.She pulled the paper out and threw it away. The clock now read 11:45."At noon,"she said to herself,"I'll move out with the crowd,and they will never see me again."

On her second attempt,Lill got through a full paragraph,but still made many mistakes.Again she pulled out the paper,threw it out and started over.This time she completed the letter,but her work was still strewn with errors.She looked at the clock:11:55—five minutes to freedom.

Just then,the door at one end of the office opened and Margaret walked in.She came directly over to Lill,putting one hand on the desk and the other on the girl's shoulder.She read the letter and paused. Then she said,"Lill,you're doing good work! "

Lill was stunned.She looked at the letter,then up at Margaret. With those simple words of encouragement,her desire to escape vanished and her confidence began to grow.She thought,"Well,if she thinks it's good,then it must be good.I think I'll stay！"

Lill did stay at Carhartt Overall Company...for 51 years,through two world wars and a Depression,through 11 presidents and six prime ministers—all because someone had the insight to give a shy

错,说成19岁。玛格丽特知道这女孩说的话里有问题,但还是决定给她一次机会。

她领着莉莲穿过卡尔特公司一间陈旧的办公室。一排又一排的人坐在一排又一排的打字机和计算器前,莉莲觉得有上百双眼睛盯着自己。这个乡下女孩羞得下巴抵到了胸前,两眼盯着地面,不情愿地跟着玛格丽特来到那间昏暗的办公室后排。玛格丽特安排她坐到一台打字机前,对她说:"莉莲,让我们见识一下你的真本事吧。"

她给了莉莲一封信让她打出来,随后就走了。莉莲看了看钟,是上午11:40,马上就该吃午饭了。她寻思到时就可以混在人群中溜掉,不过她觉得自己起码应该试试那封信。

第一次,她打了一行,5个单词,她打错了4个。她把那张纸抽出来扔掉。时钟指向11:45。"到了中午,"她自言自语道,"我就和这些人一起出去,然后他们再也不会见到我了。"

第二次,她打了整整一段,但还是错了很多。她又把那张纸抽出来扔掉,然后重新开始。这次她把信打完了,可还是满篇错误。她看看钟:11:55,再过5分钟就自由了。

就在这时,办公室另一头的门开了,玛格丽特走了进来。她直接走向莉莲,一只手放在桌子上,一只手搭在莉莲肩上。开始读莉莲打的那封信,她读完以后,停顿了一下,然后说:"莉莲,你打得真不错！"

莉莲目瞪口呆。她看看那封信,又抬头看看玛格丽特。就因为这句简单的鼓励,她想要逃跑的念头消失了,信心也开始增长。她心想:"啊,如果她认为这样算打得不错,那就一定是不错了！我看我就留下来吧！"

莉莲果然在卡尔特服装公司留了下来……而且一留就是51年,其间经历了两次世界大战,一次经济大萧条,(美国)换了11任总统,(加拿大)换了6位总理——这都是因为有人能慧眼识英雄,愿意在一个羞怯、缺乏

and uncertain young girl the gift of self-esteem when she knocked on the door.

Dedicated to Lillian Kennedy by James M.Kennedy(son)
and James C.Kennedy(grandson)

自信的年轻女孩来敲门时,帮助她恢复自尊心。

献给莉莲·甘迈迪
(子)詹姆士·M·甘迈迪和(孙)詹姆士·C·甘迈迪

The Scrapbook
剪贴簿

Life is to be fortified by many friendships. To love and to be loved is the greatest happiness.

Sydney Smith

生命需要很多友情来加固。爱与被爱都是最大的幸福。

雪莉·史密斯

Teaching English in Japan has been incredibly rewarding. I came here out of a longing for adventure and travel, and for a little relaxation. Miraculously, I've achieved all that and more. I've traveled all over the main island of Honshu, filled the pages of five journals, read over 60 books, written four short stories, and made friends with teachers and scholars from all over the world. I've been able to receive and had the chance to give back.

But my heart lies with my students—the businessmen who are being transferred to America, the housewives who want to expand their horizons, the high school students whose fondest wish is to

在日本教英语给了我许多难以置信的回报。我当初来这里是渴望冒险与旅行，并希望放松一下自己。结果奇迹般的，我不但实现了最初的心愿，还有许多额外的收获。我游遍了本州(译者注：日本最大的岛屿)各地，写完5本日记，读了60多本书，写了4个短篇故事，还和来自世界各地的老师与教授结下了友谊。我有许多接受恩惠的机会，也有许多机会回报别人的恩惠。

但我的心思全都扑在学生身上——那些即将调往美国工作的生意

attend a university in the States.

Over the course of the year that I have taught,I've often wondered who was the student and who was the teacher.The pupils nurtured and comforted me,helping me to better understand the Japanese culture.They applauded when I struggled with my first *hiragana* letters.They accompanied me to grocery store after grocery store,where I searched for three months to find peanut butter.They showed me how to fold paper into an *origami* swan and took me on riverboat rides.They invited me to traditional tea ceremonies,and over *omisoka*,the Japanese New Year,they took me into their homes,where they prepared meals in my honor.They also took me to the temple and taught me how to select a fortune;then they quickly gathered around,crying,"You have much good fortune! You big lucky! "

The last few weeks,as I've made preparations to return home, have been jam-packed with *sayonara* parties and gifts.So many students have showered me with presents:purses of handwoven silk, jewelry boxes,designer handkerchiefs, jade earrings and gold-trimmed china plates.We've sung ourselves hoarse at *karaoke*,hugged,held hands and exchanged countless good-byes.And through it all,I've managed to keep my emotions in check.Instead,I've let *them* shed the tears while I comforted them with promises to write.

Tonight is my last night to teach,and I'm ending it on an exceptionally high note with my favorite class.They're the advanced students,and over the year,we've engaged in political discussions,learned slang,role-played and done something rare among different cultures—we've laughed at one another's jokes.

While I'm preparing for this last class,Mika,the school manager, calls me to the front lobby. I enter the room and see the staff and several students standing around,hands clasped in eager anticipation. All eyes are turned in my direction.Mika has one last gift for me.

I carefully unwrap the paper,as the presentation of the gift is as important as the gift itself.The wrapper slowly slides off,and I see that she has given me a scrapbook. She tells me she prepared it just last night after weeks of collaborating with the students.I see the red-

人、想要拓展生活领域的家庭主妇以及热切希望到美国上大学的高中生。

在我教英文的这一年里,我时常分不清谁是学生,谁是老师。我的学生不但给我帮助、给我安慰,还帮助我更深入地了解日本文化。当我很艰难地用平假名写下第一封信时,他们为我鼓掌喝彩;他们陪着我走过一家又一家杂货店,只为我花了3个月的时间才买到一瓶花生酱;他们教我做折纸手工,把纸叠成一个纸天鹅,带我去划船;他们邀我欣赏传统茶道;日本人过除夕时,他们还特地在家里做饭招待我;他们带我到庙里去,告诉我如何抽签,等我抽了签他们又很快聚过来,一起大声说:"你会好运不断,吉星高照!"

我准备回国的最后几个星期里,几乎每天都有欢送派对,我也因此收到好多礼物。学生的礼物几乎将我淹没。其中包括手工做的丝质钱包、珠宝盒、设计师设计的手帕、玉耳环、镶金边的瓷盘等。我们在卡拉OK欢唱到喉咙沙哑,尽情拥抱、握手、互道无数次再见。在整个过程当中,我一直很小心控制自己的情绪,结果流泪的反而是我的学生,我则安慰他们说,我一定会写信给他们。

今晚是我最后一堂课,我和我最喜爱的一班学生共聚,准备为这段教学生涯来个最高潮。这班学生是高级生,过去一年来,我们讨论过不少政治问题,学过不少俚语。演过很多戏,还做过文化背景不同的人很少做的一件事——轮流说笑话,对对方的笑话大笑不止。

我正在为这最后一堂课做准备时,学校主任美加叫我到大厅去。我一走进大厅就看见许多同事、学生围成一圈,热烈鼓掌,每个人的目光都集中在我身上,原来美加还有最后一个礼物要给我。

我小心翼翼地拆开礼物包装,因为礼物的外表就和礼物本身一样重要。包装纸缓缓展开后,我看出美加给我的是一只剪贴簿。她说她和学生们协同合作了好几个星期。到昨天晚上才准备好这份礼物。我看见她的眼

ness in her eyes.I open the cover.

Filling the pages are recent snapshots of all my students.Beside the pictures are personal notes written by them on small,colorful squares of paper.They've decorated the papers with hearts,smiles,little cat faces and neon-colored lines,stars,dots and triangles.

I know the challenge my students face in stringing together even simple phrases,and as I read,the dam of emotions I've been holding back begins to crack.

Thank you for your kindly teach.

I had interesting class.Now maybe someday I go to America.

I am forget to you.

I've been enjoying to study English.

Thank you for everything you did me.I very sad you go to America.

Please don't forget memories in Japan.

My tears begin to fall.I grope for words that have flowed so easily over the last year.My hands lightly touch the pages,and I outline their faces with my fingertips.I close the cover and wrap the book in my arms,holding it tightly to my heart.

The scrapbook has captured them forever.I may be leaving,but I'm taking each one of them back with me to America.

Gina Maria Jerome

眶慢慢红了起来,赶紧低头拆开剪贴簿。

剪贴簿里贴满了我所有学生的近照,每张照片旁边,还有各自用小小的色彩鲜艳的方块纸写下的个人祝福。整本剪贴簿里,到处都是心形、微笑、小猫脸、霓虹七彩的线条、星星、点点和三角形等各种装饰图案。

我知道这些句子虽然简单,但学生写起来一定还是很辛苦的。我细细咀嚼每个句子,心中原本勉强抑制的情感大堤也随之溃决了。

感谢您的亲切的教导。

我觉得上课很有趣,说不定有一天我可以去美国。

我是不会忘记你的。

我很喜欢学英文。

谢谢你为我做的一切,我很难过你要回美国。

请别忘记日本的回忆。

我的泪水夺眶而出。我试着想说一些过去一年来很容易就脱口而出的话语。我的双手轻抚剪贴簿,用指尖画出每个人的脸。我把剪贴簿合上,用双手紧抱在胸前。

那本剪贴簿留下了他们永恒的记忆。我仍将离开,但我要带着他们每个人一起回美国去。

生命的彩虹